Forgotten Heroines

The diaries of Ysabel Birkbeck,
ambulance driver on the Romanian Front,
1916 - 17

Published by lulu.com 2011

Second edition, 2017

ISBN 978-1-291-62975-0

Thank you to Ysabel's son, Neil Hunter, for his permission to publish her diaries in this form.

For this second edition, my transcription has been corrected using Birkbeck's own typescript, lodged by her, along with all her other diaries from WWI and WWII and her 'mechanics notebook', in the Imperial War Museum. These Russian diaries have now joined the others, but it may be some time before they are available for study, as considerable conservation work will be needed. In a number of places, Birbeck had added information to the typescript; I've marked these. In particular, the episode of being bombed (Saturday, 14th October) was considerably expanded – that section was hard to read, so I imagined Birbeck dictating, and adding more detail as she did so.

Forgotten Heroines

The diaries of Ysabel Birkbeck,
Ambulance driver on the Romanian Front,
1916 - 17

Transcribed and edited by
Douglas Gordon Baxter
and
Marsali Taylor

When I was a child, there were old ladies who remembered the Great War. They dressed in calf-length tweed skirts with matching jumpers, thick stockings and court shoes. They smelt of face powder, had their hair set once a fortnight and played whist.

Then there was our aunt by courtesy, Ysabel Birkbeck. Aunt Ysabel lived in the cottage three miles more remote than ours; her brother's son owned the estate. She had snow-white hair that stood out in a halo around her head, and wore wide trousers, a faded navy smock with two pockets and rope-soled canvas shoes. She leant on a wooden walking stick, handle polished with use, but travelled mostly by boat, a heavy white and blue clinker dinghy called *Mine*. She bathed in the burn that ran by Caolas Mor, and left her kitchen window open to let the wild birds fly in. There was a row of perfect sea urchins along the sitting room mantelpiece, olive and coral, graded from pinky-nail small at the ends to grapefruit-sized in the middle, and her own vividly-coloured paintings of fungi hung on the walls. She had a toy rabbit, Percy, who had his own suitcase of handmade clothes: a tweed suit with a handkerchief in the breast pocket, a tailored shirt, and striped pyjamas. Well-behaved children were allowed to invite Percy to stay with them for the night. In Edinburgh, she hosted egg hunting parties at Easter. When she smiled, her round face had a thousand wrinkles.

With Aunt Ysabel, no task was impossible. I remember helping build a new landing place for *Mine*. She'd rolled a line of boulders and was filling behind them with buckets of stones. 'Go on till you can't do any more,' she said, 'then do another hundred bucketfuls.' Somehow, with her eye on you, you could.

(Voice-over by Marsali Taylor, for film *Ysabel's War*, Philip Taylor, 2008)

Aunt Ysabel and I playing draughts at Loch Hourn.
Photograph, 1967, Douglas Gordon Baxter

I liked listening to my old ladies' stories, but I never thought of asking Aunt Ysabel about her past; she was too busy living in the present. She'd been dead almost thirty years when I learned that she'd driven an ambulance on the Romanian Front in 1916. She'd been part of Elsie Inglis's Scottish Women's Unit, attached to the First Serbian Division. Like many others in the Unit Ysabel Birkbeck kept a diary ...

"All that we see or seem,
Is but a dream — within a dream —"

Please return to:

Mrs Digby
Highfield
Fakenham
Norfolk
England.

To The Scottish Women's Field Hospital.

Luck' to thee out in the day.
When the night lies behind
And to blow that makes free must be struck
Heaven send thee luck.

Peace to thee out in the night
when thou failest to find
In the roar of the wind
Woman thy feet
Oh her breast
Earth give thee rest.   G Cartwright

Aug 26 — Dec 15 - 1916.

"Think that this day will never dawn again
(Some comfort in that)

The inside cover of the first diary.

8

"All that we see or seem,
Is but a dream – within a dream."

Please return to:
Mrs Digby
Highfield,
Fakenham
Norfolk
England.

To the Scottish Women's Field Hospital
Luck to thee out in the day,
When the night lies behind
And the blow that makes free must be struck,
    Heaven send thee luck.

Peace to thee out in the night
When thou failest to find
In the roar of the wind
Way for the feet,
    On her breast,
    Earth give thee rest.
                S[1] Carlyon

Aug 26 – Dec 15 1916

"Think that this day will never dawn again."
(Some comfort in that)

---

[1] Carlyon was Charlotte Carlyon, Chauffeur from August 1916 to January 1917. However, the initial doesn't look like a C – perhaps S Carlyon was the family poet.

A loose page from the diary. The caption reads, 'Before falling among the Scottish Women.' She was now twenty-six, so the teenage photo is her sense of humour coming out. The swastika was the SWH method of marking baggage – at that time, it had no Nazi overtones.

The Ford is my car
I shall not want another [ ].

A diary of a Ford Car Start.

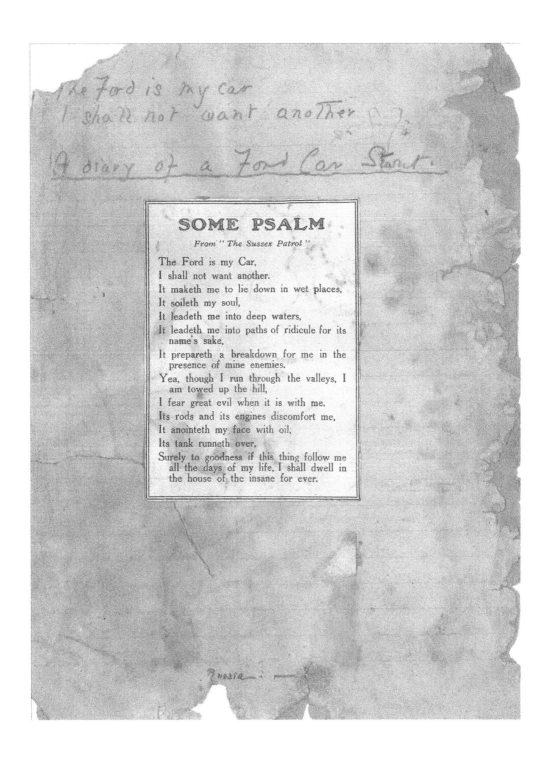

SOME PSALM

From "The Sussex Patrol"

The Ford is my Car,
I shall not want another.
It maketh me to lie down in wet places,
It soileth my soul,
It leadeth me into deep waters,
It leadeth me into paths of ridicule for its name's sake,
It prepareth a breakdown for me in the presence of mine enemies.
Yea, though I run through the valleys, I am towed up the hill,
I fear great evil when it is with me.
Its rods and its engines discomfort me,
It anointeth my face with oil,
Its tank runneth over,
Surely to goodness if this thing follow me all the days of my life, I shall dwell in the house of the insane for ever.

Russia.

11

1. The Unit assembles.

1. The Unit assembles.

When World War I was declared, the women of the suffrage societies, then still fighting for the vote, were anxious to be of use. Dr Elsie Inglis, Honorary Secretary of both the Edinburgh Women's Suffrage Society and the Scottish Federation of the National Union of Women's Suffrage Societies, offered Dr Frederick Treves of the War Office a hospital staffed by women doctors. His reply was, "My good woman, go home and be still." Inglis applied to the N.U.W.S.S. for funding for a women's unit, and the Scottish Women's Hospitals for Foreign Service was formed. Their first hospital was at Royaumont, near Paris, under the auspices of the French Red Cross, and the first mobile unit was attached to the Serbian Army. In all, over a thousand women were to serve as doctors, nurses, orderlies and ambulance drivers with the S.W.H. When the Serbian troops were ordered to the Romanian Front in the summer of 1916, a new mobile unit was formed. This unit consisted of seventy-five women, including the 25-strong Transport under Mrs Evelina Haverfield, a militant suffragette who'd stood trial with Mrs Pankhurst. Ysabel Birkbeck, then aged 26, was officially the Driving Instructor for the Transport.

The Unit which went out in August 1916 was designed to form two smaller Field units. It consisted of:
Four doctors: Dr Inglis, Dr Chesney, Dr Corbett and Dr Potter.
Two Matrons, Fox and Vizard.
Twenty trained nurses (the diarists call them sisters): Atkinson, Bangham, Cliver, Cunningham, Edwards, Gilchrist, Grant, Henderson, Hopkin, Jackson, Jenkins F, Jenkins S, Kinnaird, Lewis, Little, McElhone, Mundie, Ulph, Walker-Brown and Wilcox.
Administrator: Henderson. Clerk: Wotherspoon.
Chief cook: Milne; Assistant cook: Ford.
Laundry Supervisors: Broadbent, Clack - assisted by David, a soldier, who was the laundry orderly.
Sanitary Inspector: Pleister.
Two Medical Students: Murphy A, Rendel.
Thirteen orderlies: Bell, Bowerman, Brand, Brown, Currie, Fawcett, Fitzroy, Johnson, Kent, Mackenzie A, Moir, Sedgewick, Turner.

The Medical students, orderlies and Transport Unit were all unpaid volunteers.

The Transport Unit

Haverfield, Evelina
Transport Officer

Birbeck, Ysabel
Driving Instructor

Carlyon, Charlotte

Clibborn, Dorothy M

Cunningham, Arminella

Donisthrope, Francis E

Ellis, Winifred

Faithfull, Edith O

Glubb, Gwenda M

Onslow, Alexandrina, left and Hedges, Geraldine. These two both did two stints in Russia, Aug 1916 – March 1917, and June – November, 1917. Hedges' third spell was as Transport Officer, Feb – Nov 1918

Hodges, Katherine M

Holme, Vera, had been driver to the Pankhurst family

.

MacDougall, Mattie J

MacGuire, Mary E

Jensen, Gladys S

Livesay, Dorothy B

Mackenzie-Edwards, Hester

Plimsoll, Ruth W

Reaney, Mabel J

Walker, Patricia

as well as **Gartleen, Eveleen; Monfries, Helen; Murphy, Clare M; Robinson, E Frances:** and cooks Suche, **Geraldine K,** and Hamner, **Helen C.**

In November 1916, they were joined by **Marx, C Margaret.** (left), and two male mechanics, **Day, George H,** and **Cowland, Percy.**

London to Liverpool

Birkbeck's diary begins on 24th August 1916, with members of the Unit assembling in London to drive the cars and lorries from Brighton to Liverpool. The Transport wore khaki, and so became known as 'the Buffs', in contrast to 'the Greys'. Several diarists commented on how smart the Transport looked, and how masculine, with their short hair, which they'd already had cut (by their brothers' barbers, by the looks of them). The Greys were later to follow their example, and in Romania both Buffs and Greys wore breeches, initially under their calf-length skirts.

Saturday 26th August 1916 – London.

Spent the morning buying last luxuries – packed, washed etc. Sybil helped.[1] At 12.30 we were at Victoria Station where I had to meet others of my Unit who were also going to Brighton to bring down cars. It was very amusing getting a first glimpse of my companions. Most were dressed in rather ascratch collection of uniforms. I myself had no tunic but only my khaki garage coat. Mrs Haverfield came early and at last we got off. Six in my carriage, mostly W.R.A[2], who saluted and sirred till I wondered what I ought to do. The cars were all more or less ready, eight ambulances and two touring cars. We moved off separately as we were ready, I first, at about 3.30 with vague instructions to go by Worthing (quite wrong). I went on by Horsham and found myself at last in Balham High St in pouring rain at about 7 after having been utterly stupid about the road. After Wandsworth and Battersea Bridge I went along to Holland Gate tGarage to find two others had arrived before me. We hung about till 8 when I rushed back to the Burlington to find Morton, Sylvia and Poppy awaiting me. We went on to the Palladium and had a box after I had fed.

Sunday 27th August

Collected at the garage at 9. Pouring rain. The others all moved off to muster at Waterloo Place, in an absolute downpour. I was left on the touring car to see what could be done to one of the ambulances that would not start. A kind man helped for four hours and we got off at last. Sybil turned up and came with all that were left of us to lunch, then off we went in earnest. An unpromising start – drenched - cold and miles behind. All went well once we got fairly going, and we picked up the others at St Albans. We drove very slowly with many stops, and eventually crawled into Birmingham at about 11.30. I had been put on one car after another, that was pulling badly or on strike. Luckily for my reputation I came across nothing more serious than an over-oiled commutator, plugs sucking, oil short-circuiting and wrongly adjusted carburetter. Birmingham was <u>pitch</u> I drove R's car[3] in - R in the last stages of fatigue and bleating weakly that we had no tail lights and neither had the car ahead. That was all too true. As I had already got her mixture correct earlier in the day and had been put back on the car because she had altered it again, I was feeling rather short. Soaked drill uniform – after driving all day – is apt to be depressing towards midnight without repeated reminders that we were in danger from front and rear as well. We got separated in Birmingham – some going to one garage, some to another – and we had no sooner fitted our cars in, than we had to go to the other garage. Oiling, greasing, washing and filling up took us till 12.30 – I had a tube to change and left the garage with the last. The hunt that followed for the 'Hen and Chickens' will be a nightmare to all of us others for ages. <u>Pitch</u> dark streets

---

[1] Sybil was her sister-in-law, wife of her oldest brother, Henry.
[2] Women's Reserve Ambulance
[3] Reaney or Robinson.

and drizzling rain and not a soul to ask for directions. When we arrived we had a scratch meal, tea, bread and jam, and found we could turn in next door. There most of the transport were already sleeping like tops, on the floor, with their heads pillowed on their rucksacks. I lay down too but could not sleep for wondering what was ahead.

Monday 28th August.

On the road by 5, as dawn broke. A very spruce, cheerful party considering, I thought. We drove without food till 8 when we reached Stafford and had a huge breakfast. R's car running perfectly. I was shifted about again, not getting back to Royce[1] once, till it began missing (over-oiled). I had a puncture, and assisted in a breakdown that took ages, and got thoroughly left on Hedges' car, with MacDougall's that I had just put right behind - so we raced, and went all round via Warrington, where we shook off the others, to Liverpool. There we found the touring cars and were caught by MacDougall and sailed up to the Exchange Hotel - to find the party we thought so far ahead, we had somehow passed. A wearing afternoon on the docks preparing cars for packing and <u>then</u> a meal. I went right to bed till dinner. After dinner we all went to a pretty entertaining variety show – we had a bench to ourselves. Included an atrocious topical song sung by a vulgar ..?

Tuesday 29th August

Lots of last shopping.

Wednesday 30th August

All aboard by 3.

---

[1] Car no 8's name.

2. The journey to Medgidia

2. The journey to Medgidia

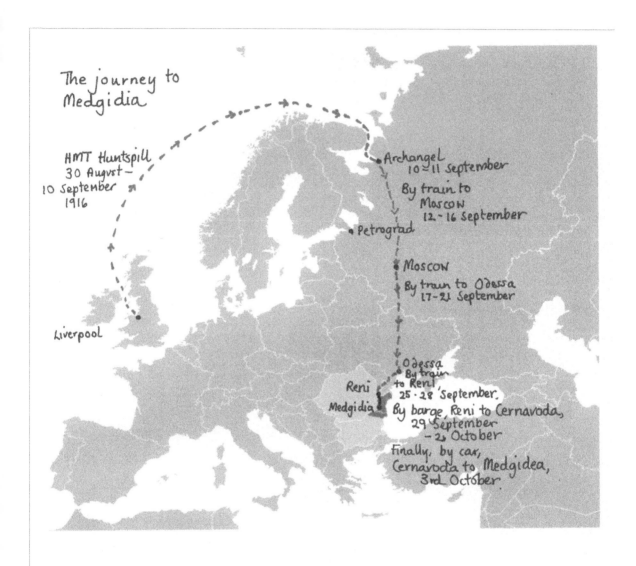

The journey to Medgidia

HMT Huntspill
30 August –
10 September
1916

Liverpool

Archangel
10–11 September

By train to
Moscow
12–16 September

Petrograd

Moscow

By train to Odessa
17–21 September

Odessa
By train
to Reni
25–28 September.

Reni

Medgidia

By barge, Reni to Cernavoda,
29 September
– 2 October

Finally, by car,
Cernavoda to Medgidea,
3rd October.

Aboard HMT *Huntspill*

Wednesday 30th August to Sunday 10th September

HMT *Huntspill* was an Austrian Lloyd, captured at the beginning of the war, and used since as a troopship in the Mediterranean. All but the engineer were new aboard her, and when the women arrived the ship was 'filthy', Dr Inglis reported, and the crew 'drunk to a man.' Mrs Haverfield's comment was that 'the only way to get this ship right was to get her <u>out.</u>'

Huntspill later sank at her moorings at Ocean Quay, Southampton Dock. The official verdict was cause unknown, but sabotage was suspected.

Thursday 31st August

One of my cabin companions was extremely ill so I got leave to sleep in one of the boats on the boat deck. Glubb and I made ourselves very comfortable in our boat with rugs and coats. The night was lovely and the ship rolled till every star was a shooting star. Nearly everyone else was ill. We probably would have succumbed also if we had been below. As it was, we loved it.

Friday – Saturday, 1st 2nd September

Much the same. The ill ones reappearing. Violent friendships were formed and as fiercely broken but it was never for a moment the least like an ordinary voyage. Drill, Swedish and otherwise, took place every morning and language classes helped to fill up the time. My lecture on a Ford ambulance was thinly attended first time, but the audiences grew. Yesterday Mrs Haverfield came and we skimmed through everything. Care, ignition, carburettor, in theory. To-day I shall take down a carburettor. Some know nothing at all, others I dare say more than I do. It makes one smile when I think how lately I met my first Ford ambulance – some of the others have been on them months and all listen open-mouthed to my teaching. I wish I had to give a lecture on the lorries, I could talk about ordinary magnetos, etc.

Livesay and Birkbeck on board ship.

One of the sketches from Birkbeck's notes for her lectures, and, overleaf, pages from the notebook.

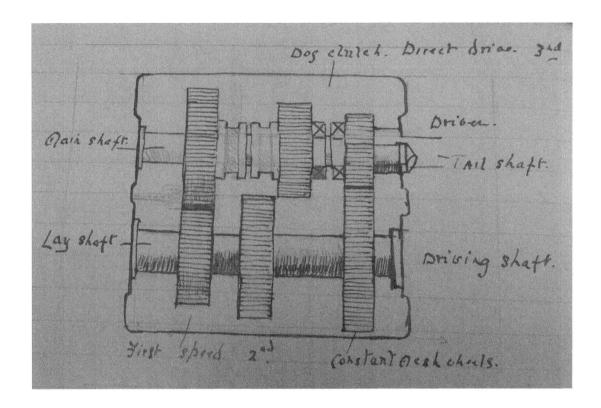

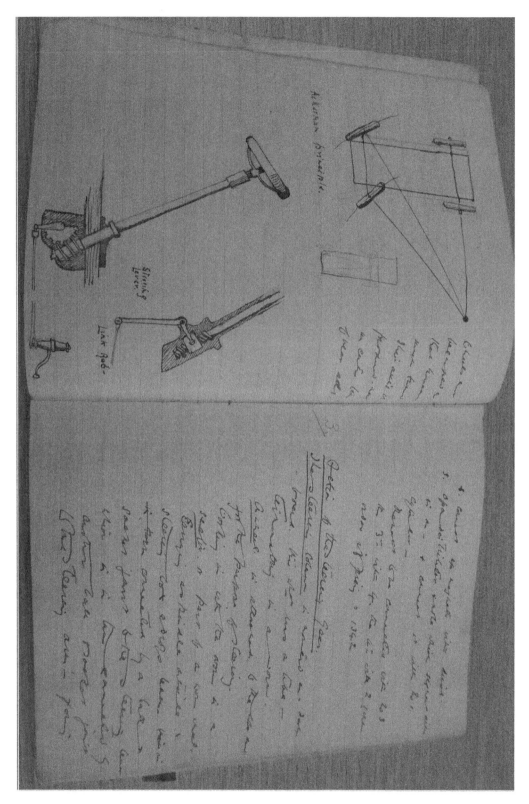

Sunday 3rd September

Church parade at 11. A boiling hot day. We lay in rows about the ship basking in the sun. Not a thing has been seen since we left the coast of Ireland behind, except a submarine last night.

Glubb, Jensen, Birkbeck (with ship's cat), Walker and two Serbian officers.

Boat drill - Three bleats of the siren and we all leap into lifebelts and gallop to our respective boats - I have a Gieve[1] waistcoat which affords a lot of amusement on these occasions. Usually after dinner we collect in a music saloon and sing part songs. The one or two Serbian officers join us, and sometimes bring some of their men with them. One with a wonderful voice sits and sings on and on, his men accompanying him with chords. It was the most wonderful effect and had a depth and richness that made other singing cheap and thin. How sad their songs were. Serbia! The work means more every day. But - how many days there are – and what a length. Night, under a pile of rugs, dressed in shirt and breeches, fleece undercoat and woolly thick stockings, over all my sleeping bag lightly tucked in. I have never once been cold, although now we are in Arctic seas, and it's so cold at daybreak it takes courage to face the decks. The Northern lights are a new wonder.

---

[1] `Patented by Navy tailors Gieve. It looked like a normal black waistcoat, but had an inflatible middle section.

Friday 8th September

We had a fancy dress dance to celebrate the end of the voyage. Considering that we none of us had anything except pyjamas and uniform it was amazing what people appeared in. The costumes ranged from an Early Victorian – Little Willie – Tweedle Dee – and a cow boy. I could rise no higher than Puss in Boots with wire whiskers stuck through a soft Balaclava helmet and wearing my jacket and field boots and at the beginning of the evening a rope tail.

Saturday 9ᵗʰ September

Woke to find a thin brown strip of land along the right side of the boat. A low brown bank - Russia at last. Land soon appeared on the other side too, a faint line growing more and more definite till on both sides were a fringe of fir trees growing to the edge of the sea. That night we stayed outside Archangel, and Plimsoll and I had our last prowl after supper. It was a heavenly night. We climbed up to the crossbar and sat and talked until it became too cold, when we climbed down we sat over the steam boiler till we were warm enough to go to bed – on deck.

Douglas Gordon Baxter, 1991:

She had found herself then, in London, where in that curious unreal atmosphere of tumult and excitement, despite or because of what lay ahead, she arrived to take up war work, doing what others of her aquaintance did, voluntary work, first aid, hospital auxiliary, Red Cross work, anything to help, but it was not until about a year later that she found her niche, you might say, and accompanied by Royce, their metier. The Scottish Women's Hospital was fitting out a detachment for Russia and looking for volunteer transport drivers. That this should have appealed to her might not seem obvious at a glance, and how this felicitous coming together of so much that was complementary is unexplained, nor did she refer to it, but the fact remians there were connections between Norfolk and Russia, because over the years governesses had gone there and some had lived in the semi-oriental splendour of Grand Ducal palaces, and written about it, so she may have heard already at first, or second hand, stories of this great, still, mysterious land, stories of snow and the taiga, endless dark birch forests to the horizon, of troikas and droshkies, of tinkling sleigh bells and brightly caparisoned horses skilfully managed by their huge padded, blue coated kuchars, the sudden onrush of the magical Russian spring and immense blue summer skies across fields of wild flowers and undulating meadowgrass, of indolent boyars and their moujiks living out the seasons in a style reminiscent of the Très Riches Heures of the Duc du Berry, in dreamlike Oblomovkaland. It must have seemed irrestible to a young woman of spirit, already something of an expert on the hugest truly oriental country of them all,[1] not to want to go, with Royce this time, not walking, she had done that, walking was out, to its near neighbour and an ally, Russia, and make common cause against the enemy.

---

[1] She had spent the first six months of 1909 travelling with her mother and sister Judith, to visit her oldest sister Gillian, a missionary in Japan. Mrs Birkbeck and Judith had been carried through China by litter, with Ysabel walking behind, 'eyes fixed,' she later said, 'on the pigtail of the nearest Chinaman.' Her diaries of this visit are in the University of Durham.

Marsali Taylor, 2011

I first took an interest in the diaries when Mum was visited by Audrey Fawcett Cahill, grand-daughter of the Fawcett of the diaries, then researching her meticulous history of the S.W.H's time in Romania, *Between the Lines* (The Pentland Press Ltd, 1999). When the book was published, there was an exhibition in Surgeon's Hall, Edinburgh, and the diaries were there, open at the drawings of "Shelling ahead" and the unit hauling the kitchen car uphill. I wish I could go back to those displays now, knowing the people, and look properly. Back at the house, I sped through Mum's neat, even typescript, fascinated by the sudden switches from dogged, appalling journeys to flirting with officers. Then I read Dr Cahill's book, which made sense of the whole campaign – except that the typescript continued with Aunt Ysabel, Turner and Edwards returning to Reni from revolutionary Petrograd to rejoin their unit, a reunion with Royce, and the journey home with the dying Elsie Inglis. It ended with Aunt Ysabel's account of Dr Inglis's funeral in St Giles, Edinburgh, and memorial service in Westminster Abbey.

'How come,' I asked Mum, 'Dr Cahill doesn't mention Aunt Ysabel going back to the Unit? Didn't Dad give Dr Cahill that bit?'

'Oh, she was very excited about that,' Mum said, 'because nobody knew how they'd got home to England. But Dad thought there should be an ending, so he added that bit.'

My academic soul was outraged. 'He *wrote* it?' Without even a note to say where the diaries ended and his fiction began?

Once I looked, of course, I could make a fair guess. Dad modelled his style on Proust, losing himself (and me) in flowing phrases, completely unlike Aunt Ysabel's clear, terse style. Her last entry seemed to be in Petrograd, on the 18th of March, in the thick of the Russian Revolution.

All the same, I wanted to know. When the diaries returned from the exhibition, I took them home to Shetland to see for myself.

The progress of the war in 1916:

Conscription had now been introduced. After the indecisive Battle of Jutland on 31 May, Allied shipping losses were increasing. Lord Kitchener and his staff were killed by a mine off Orkney on 5 June, and Lloyd George replaced Kitchener as Secretary of State for War. Casulties from the on-going Somme offensive were heavy.

On the Russian front, however, Galicia had been regained, and this success induced Romania to join the Allied forces on the 27th August. This gave the Allies a Black Sea port, Constanta, but also extended the front the Russians were defending. Romania's other borders all edged hostile powers - Austro-Hungary, Bulgaria and occupied Serbia - and the Turkish fleet, reinforced by German destroyers, patrolled her coast.

The Dobruja province was bordered by the Black Sea to the east, and the marsh-delta of the Danube to north and west. It had been part of Bulgaria till 1913. Romania's main rail links were westwards, to Bucharest; to go to and from Russia, passengers and freight had to change trains at Reni, because the Russian engines were of a wider gauge than the Romanian, and this, along with the single-track system, had implications for troop and refugee movement. The vital link between Constanta and the west was the Carol Bridge, one of the longest iron railway bridges in the world at that time. Cernavoda was on the eastern end of the bridge, and the railway continued east through Medgidia to Constanta.

The Central forces were then pushing northwards from the Bulgarian border, and General Alekseev sent two infantry divisions and one cavalry division, 50,000 men in total, under the command of General Grutskovsky, to defend the border. 14,000 of them were Southern Slavs of the First Serbian Division, to which the Scottish Women's Hospital was attached, and so it was at Medgidia that the first hospital was to be set up, less than twenty miles from the front.

By train, barge and car to Medgidia.

Archangel
10–11 September

By train to
Moscow
12–16 September

Petrograd

Moscow

By train to Odessa
17–21 September

Odessa
By train
to Reni
25–28 September.

Reni

Medgidia

By barge, Reni to Cernavoda,
29 September
– 2 October

Finally, by car,
Cernavoda to Medgidea,
3rd October.

Archangel, and by train to Moscow.

Sunday, Monday 10th and 11th September

We spent two days at Archangel. As we arrived a British Motor Launch, belonging to the Transport people, came up with, as we afterwards learnt, one Mr Charles in charge. We went ashore next day. It was so nice to get off for a proper walk. It was like Norway. Stacks and stacks of wood. The whole place smelt of it, deliciously. It was a disappointing place, and looked as if it had been quickly built, two days before, and might be as quickly removed. We all trooped about in a herd. Next day Suche and I went there alone, by ferry, and enjoyed it much better. It was easier then to realise that Peter the Great had been there and that it was of huge importance. We had tea at the Café de Paris and found English and French both easily understood. We had tea and bread and butter, no cakes. Then returned by the *Blackcock* to the boat with several others and all the Navy transport people, and all other English men, and several Russian officers came to dine, as usual, and we had the usual sing-song after, followed by supper in the pantry for the chosen.

Tuesday 12th September

Another day in Archangel. Roll call after a day in Archangel, rather an amusing finish. The *Blackcock* started as late as it could and passed the conscientious ferry ploughing along. We of the T.C. just got in in time. The usual crowd accompanying us, Charles, Morris, Macbeth, Captain Scott, Helmsley[1] – who has a lovely voice. A lot of Russians from the next ship (a troop ship) came too. We were ordered to get ready to start at 8pm and hang all our small luggage about our persons. I found it a goodly burden. For myself I was weighed down by my great coat plus its fleece lining, rug rolled up and slung across one shoulder, haversack and water bottle – oily stuffed through the straps - and in my hand a canvas bucket in which an orange melon lay balanced on top of my change - and so forth. Charlie our marvellous steward gave it me as we left.

Our on-off departure was put off again and again. We filled up the time with songs and choruses, Tipperary, John Brown's Body, the Long Trail, Keep the Home Fires burning and others. At 11 pm came the order to go. We were lined up outside the ship, formed fours and marched to the train. The Ship's Band – formed of firemen and stokers – fell in behind playing 'It's a long way to Tipperary'. We sang vigorously till roars of cheers drowned our song. Hundreds of Russian soldiers, which we had not seen in the dark, were massed on

---

[1]   None of them are SWH women. – officers of the *Blackcock*, perhaps.

either side of our way. They cheered as I have never heard men cheer, and went on and on long after we were all fitted into the train - all 75 of us. Our friends had come with us, and helped us settle in. We gradually took in all the discomfort of the train. First we found there was no light but a two-inch candle on the wall. The Russians gave up cheering and sang. Mrs Reti and Captain Scott came and joined Suche[1] and me in our cabin and talked till 2 in the morning. Then at last the whistle blew as if it meant it. The Ship's Band redoubled its efforts and the Russians cheered again. As the train crawled away we heard their cheers grow fainter and fainter, and so we started on the next stage of our journey - I don't think anyone there that night will ever forget it.

Wednesday 13th September

No blankets, no water, no lights and no heating, and the noisiest, jerkiest train in the world, combined to give us a pretty cheerless night, but I slept. Rations, bread and cheese, were brought round at 8.30 by the kitchen orderlies. Suche and I made quite a good job of it, with hot tea - cooked on my stove – and melon – and sardines. We soon got warm. Forest grew up to the line on either side, fir and silver birch, with an occasional flash of crimson mountain ash in the clearings. A cheerful rumour of a hot meal at 2 reached us – a rumour it remained though – till most had gone to bed hungry. We were turned out at 2 am at Bacheridza[2] where we had an excellent supper, hot soup, meat and fish, and best of all delicious Russian tea, with lemon. The train stopped continually and we exercised and amused ourselves after dark by dropping off and on the train and running by the side whenever the train went slow enough, which was very often. I stumbled and lost one of my slippers and daren't stop to pick it up.

So we live - Suche and I messing together, and living very peaceably.

Valogda.

Saturday 16th September

Moscow. We expected to arrive at 7 and were ready. However the train shunted around the outskirts for seven hours, before we actually arrived. Exasperating. Here we had a first glimpse of the war. Part of the hotel was a sort of sorting hospital, and wounded and Red Cross were everywhere. Then we marched to a hotel for lunch, which we did not get over till 4.

---

[1] Suche, Geraldine, was the cook attached to the Transport.
[2] Gap left for name. Bacheridza is DGB's suggestion.

At last we proceeded to the Kremlin just as the sun was going down, and there I saw enough to know that one half had not been told. My history was too weak to appreciate the historical interest, but one needed no prompting to appreciate the wealth of golden domes against the sky. A dream place and more impressive than anything I had ever seen – gateways – and then, into the cathedral in the half dark to hear Russian church music then home – past a group of guns taken at Premseli, and so through streets where one longed to get lost – back in the dark to the station. I'm full of plans now for Moscow, after this work has been finished. Perhaps as a chauffeur, cook or teacher of English. Two hours in the Kremlin, what can you do in two hours, as a member of a unit that orders you to form fours and marches you off, past where Ivan the Terrible walked, an object of pity and derision to oneself at least.

This time I was too busy to mind. Flu or the worst kind of cold – earache, neuralgia and throat - has gone through the train. I have had it to the full, so a good deal has been missed.

By train from Moscow to Odessa.

Sunday 17th September

A lovely day. The train crawled for two hours in the morning. We stopped, and most of the Transport climbed on to the trucks at the back of the train and spent the day there. For the first time I really loved the country. Quite flat and lovely colour, patches of dark bluish ploughed land, rye I suppose, and patches of sunflowers. The sky seems more important here than anywhere else in the world – and far bigger! Huge woolly clouds across a clear, rather sharp blue. I lay on my front on the truck and watched them and the horizon changing.

Tea parties and supper parties are the fashion. The food supplied by the unit is mostly sufficient to nourish - but not to amuse. There is a rush at the stations, of buffs, greys and Serbians, all buying buns, fruit and feverishly filling water bottles at the boilers to be found at every Russian station. We supplement our rations by anything we can find.

On Sunday 17th September, Milne, the Head Cook, invited Birkbeck and Suche to tea. She called them "such jolly girls" and said that Birkbeck had promised to teach her to drive her kitchen car.

Wednesday 20th September

Stopped early at Tcherkass and remained there all day. It was a great Red Cross centre. Many trains were in the station, all beautifully clean, either empty or carrying wounded. The nurses were very attractive in spotless white caps and aprons, and grey frocks. We had leave from 10 to 1.15 so Suche and I went right afield in the country, and enjoyed ourselves hugely too. After following a track across a dry plain for some way, we came to some trenches – then further to a swamp where all kinds of flowers grew. We put up a hawk quite close, and it hovered over us in cool contempt. As we lay on our backs in the sun we discovered dozens of little lizards dodging about in the grass. It was such a peaceful day away from the unit.

Back by 1 to lunch in the restaurant with real appetites.

We had a supper party for ten in our cabin, and fed them off sandwiches, chicken, and things bought at the station. We played games after, till our guests departed at 10 - a late hour for this life.

Thursday 21ˢᵗ September

Woke early on another lovely day and the same lovely big country. Endless flat low grass hills in huge waves over the landscape. We stopped frequently along the line. Our Russian robber friends had been dropped and we picked up a train of recruits. As they got onboard, a woman at a little wayside station burst into tears and cried as if she'd never hope again. Too many women have cried like that and <u>still</u> the war goes on.

The rumour was – Odessa at 4. But at 4 we were watching in vain for a sight of sea, or city, and at 6 fell asleep having been changed into our kit. At 7.30 we did arrive. At O. the arrangements for us were <u>too</u> good, after Moscow. We were all put into droshkies two by two and driven off at once to our temporary home, a sanitorium. Suche and I got a room to ourselves in a little row of three. The whole compound is planted with trees and yew hedges and you really feel fairly detached. Little streets of rooms are dotted all over the place, just bungalows, with one or two main buildings. It was the height of luxury to have a room to ourselves alone with bedtable, chairs <u>and</u> water and washing stand. I wanted to go to bed at once but dinner came first, in an open dining hall, an excellent dinner too. Then bed and better almost, our kit-sacks with fresh clothes. Even my cough could not spoil my sleep, after three weeks out of bed. Our grey walls and bare floor were spotless.

Friday 22ⁿᵈ September

Up at 7.30 for the promised tub in the bathhouse. We were told there were forty baths but on arrival found one big room with five baths in it and three single ones. Everyone was clamouring for the three, one of which was cold. I with low cunning whipped into one unnoticed and spent half an hour wrestling with the grime of nine days' train. We Transport scored off the long-haird greys!

Saturday 23ʳᵈ September

Odessa does not pretend to be Russian or old, but we <u>do</u> love it. Shops – Franconi's, where you get wonderful chocolates, cakes and meals, sitting outside as in Paris – wide streets, which are crossed at the risk of one's life, cabs, trams and cars appearing at the wrong side, and just anyhow, and droshkies driven by not too expert ladies. The horses are lovely and beautifully kept. Most have Medici collars, and lots of them ornamental harness. Their drivers, always colossally fat, are dressed in full skirted coats crossed with studded belts. The droskies themselves have only room for two, if thin, and no kind of back at all. Lots of horses have no bits in their mouths.

Some English girls came to show us round and one took me to a bank where I got a cheque cashed after about two hours. The man said it was absurd to have an account for £50, although I tried to explain it was only pocket money. 1 Rouble = about £1.

Mrs Haverfield made me go and choose tools for the cars all the afternoon. Very funny. I took Jensen too and we simply walked around till we saw what we wanted and took it. Prices were absurd. There was endless sitting about which was fairly annoying.

Sunday 24th September

The Transport went to the opera and saw *La Dame de Pique* (Tchaikovsky). We arrived as the first act ended and all crept into our boxes, thoroughly ashamed. We were six to a box and had very good places in the 2nd tier. The opera house was layered up and full of bright uniforms. We recognised Spero, one of our Serbian friends who had come with us from Liverpool, and also some of the 'non coms'. During the intervals we walked about a lot, and found ourselves stared at, but kindly.

EXTRACTS FROM RUSSIAN NEWSPAPER.
++++++++++++++++++++++++++++++++++-----

Yesterday's performance at th Opera House had a very pompous character. The Grand Duchess Mary Pavlova graciously came at half past eight accompanied by the highest military and civil authorities.

The second floor of boxes was occupied by the Field Hospital and the transport of the British Red Cross staying just now in Odessa. After the end of the first act, according to Her Highness express wish, all the Scottish Red Cross nurses were invited to the foyer where the Govenor of Odessa and the British Consul General introduced the Unit to the Grand Duchess. Her Highness walked along the ranks and honoured the nurses by gracious words in English.

Birkbeck obviously wasn't impressed by the Grand Duchess, for her diary entry for the Opera visit ends there, but there's a fuller account some pages on in another hand:

24. 9. 16 The lions sat down with the lambs for the first time together at 6.30pm. The joy was intense. Private trams were waiting to take us to the Opera House. With a good deal of mock military fuss we eventually got there. Fortunately for the Grays the boxes were more

or less evenly distributed that is to say there was no box from which it was impossible to see or to hear.

The performance was indifferent.

The two chief features of the evening were the Grand Duchess Maria Pavlovna who sat in the royal box, and two portly figures who occupied a box meant for six, while the other boxes of the same size were crowded to overflowing. We regret to say that one of the figures aforementioned spent the best part of the evening in hunting.

Towards the end of the first act during a most touching part of the performance word was passed round that the Grand Duchess wished to inspect the unit.

In a few moments the door of our box was flung open with a crash and the commandant of the Buffs fell over the door and in a loud voice ordered us not to make so much noise.

We slunk from our box and joined our sisters in the foyer where we were told to line up on either side and look our plainest, which we succeeded in doing admirably. The only other order we received was that we must neither faint nor speak when the Grand Duchess looked at us.

Our brother Buffs opposite to us were looking their smartest admirably drilled by Field Marshall Holme, who was untiring in her salutes to her chief.

Our officers, ranged on the side of the Buffs, seemed to be suffering from nervous collapse, this was particularly true of one of them, we regret to say a Buff, whose lips were cracking and her fingers twitching with agitation.

At last the great lady arrived and some of the humbler greys were surprised to see officers in uniform curtsey, whereas in their humble opinion to kiss her hand would have been more in keeping.

Городской Театръ.

Антрепризà А. И. Сибирева

Having been inspected we returned to our boxes where a graceful tribute was paid to England by the singing of the National Anthem.

The rest of the performance was excessively dull and lengthy, and we were not a little glad when all was over, and we could creep back to our sofas in the friendly sanitorium.

Sunday again. Suche and I walked to the sea, about ten minutes – along a footpath, then down the cliff to the shore. Jagged rocks of pale pink stone broke the waves. We found a little bay to ourselves and sat and basked there all the morning. Dark and deep the Black Sea looked, a sea indeed. Some of the others bathe every morning, but I had not recovered from the plague sufficiently.

Monday 25th September

Our last day in Odessa. Suche and I went into the town and shopped necessities. I got some practical stores for Bell's and my lot. Prices are excessive, candles 2/- each, 7/- a tin of cocoa and so on. Milne and I met at Franconi's before starting out to lunch with the consul. We missed the Consulate of course and had to resort to a droshky. The man drove us off to the French consulate despite our protests, and we were directed again from there. Already late, we hurled our hate at his bulging back. Mr Bagg came on with us. We found two Greys there and had a very happy luncheon. It was decidedly nice to be a person again, and not a member of the unit. After lunch we hurried home to pack, not so easy, as we didn't know whether the journey was to last 24 hours, or so many days. My haversack holds enough for days and days according to our present ideas of cleanliness and the necessities of life. I carry in it, one change of clothing, pyjamas, brushes, washing things, towel, tin mug and plate, knife, fork and spoon, my little cooker, Kodak, and writing things and a book. All left at 7 and all our luggage was thrown up on a lorry by our Serbian soldier servants, and off we rumbled in a tram. At the station we went through the usual humiliations and were finally dismissed to feed in the restaurant. All the English had turned up, one with a parting gift of a coat-hanger for me. We found our old train waiting for us and old Alexander wreathed in smiles at our return. Cheers and more good-byes and then another wait before we moved out into the darkness, for what seemed the hundredth time, with goodbyes in our ears – one does nothing else these times of war.

On, and on – and on, we journeyed – more slowly now than ever, along a straight line to Reni.

It makes one feel small but terribly alive, this country. Hour after hour one sits on the step of the train watching mile after mile roll by. Dead dried-up grassland and rolling hills. Roads unmarked by stone or fence, cutting straight away to the horizon, roads are things to follow. Some slopes are cultivated, growing maize, sunflowers – and rye – near the villages – and here are trees too. Then on again for miles with no sign of life but a herd of cows, or horses attended by a boy riding a horse bareback, without bridle or halter. Then miles from anywhere a cart crawling across the landscape in a cloud of dust.

Mrs Haverfield left us at Tiraspol and went on ahead to Reni. Here we saw our troop train going to the front for the second time. We were naturally pleased to see each other. The little Russian girl and I had a long talk (French) and I persuaded her to clamber onto our train to see our cars. We gave the men cigarettes.

After lunch we got leave for two hours and Dr Potter and I went off for a walk into the town. It was very picturesque, especially the fruit market. I could not resist two pottery plates and brought one home full of lemons. A tea-party again – some people have a marvellous gift of picking up food - my hostesses had.

Thursday 28th September

Stopped at a little station where I saw more rats than one can describe, they were all bubbling out under the edge of a barn, and make expeditions to scavenge on the line. Revolting. The whole edge was writhing with them. Murphy and I armed ourselves with sticks and crept across the line and slashed about, but got none. Several dogs watched us rather cynically. I suppose they had also failed. We stood quite close in and let them get well away before we charged. We were so interested in the crusade that we only thought of the train as it began to move. We'd just time to dash under the fence and leap on. We have all learned to treat the whistle with contempt and someone must get left soon.

By barge from Reni to Cernavoda

Friday September 29th

Reni – The Danube – We arrived and spent the day unloading the train. Getting the cars down from the trucks was very exciting. The strength of the soldiers told off to help was marvellous, they lifted the cars about bodily. We each sat in ours ready to steer them down to earth. We lunched aboard a Russian boat, all ravenous, as we were depending on the food at 1 - it came at 4. Then some of us sneaked off for baths. After days on the train we were prepared to face anything. A Russian officer took us there. The only room was heated as a Turkish bath. There we waited our turn before going into the scrubbing room. We returned to hear we were leaving – the Transport to go on a barge with the cars and luggage while the Greys went in the *George*. The barge was tied up to others, carrying Russian troops and their lorries – one was carrying nothing but horses. All were towed by a gallant tug. It was dark before we had time to look for warm corners to sleep in. My car was full of cases, so I slept on deck and got frozen till Donisthorpe came at 3am and took me into her lorry. Our neighbours had an excellent breakfast and we all sniffed the delicious whiff of stew while we ate our bread. Life for us was exactly like theirs except their food was good. We washed in a bucket on deck in turn, and refilled it by a rope slung overboard. The river was a thick dull brown and we wondered who ever saw it blue. On either side a belt of huge willows hid Romania from us. Sheepskin coats were given out, and kept us fine and warm at night, but the dye came off terribly and we were all coal black in the morning.

(Left) Birkbeck and Jensen roughing it aboard the barge

Cunningham

A well on the bank.

Monday 2nd October

Three days we were on the barge, eating less and less as food became shorter and shorter. Luckily it was hot and we could lie and bask in the sun all day. Our neighbours were pretty light-fingered and used to prowl all over our barge at night till we had to put a guard all night long, on watches of three hours each. I had the 2 – 5 watch, but Donisthorpe insisted on doing it for me, because of my cough. They were peaceful days with plenty of sun and nothing to do.

We did a little to our cars the last day. In the evenings we sang choruses till we became too hungry.

The day we arrived at Cernavoda I was in a panic in case the Fords would not start, but next day to my huge relief, all did. We drove them off the barge and lined up at the quay. The troop also disembarked and camped all round. They were still more pressing in their visits, and we had four on guard, up and down the two lines till they moved off suddenly and silently at midnight. We were very hungry, and it was trying to hang about, hours, before getting an excellent meal on one of the ships. My 'watch' was 10 – 12, and we got back from supper just in time. Very eerie it was, watching there – the soldiers were hardly more than restless before we realized they were off. Lorries, cars, carts, infantry, all streamed away. One officer on a beautifully made horse was silhouetted sharp against the water and waiting to fall in jovially behind – and so they went, where? and to what fate.

Tuesday 3rd October

At 5 next morning we prepared to start and then the cars all played up. One lorry had a broken piston ring or something, another a bent needle valve and both were left behind. Eight Ford ambulances, two touring cars, two kitchens and one Selden lorry got off at 9. It had poured hard all night – most of the cars had leaked, and we were a pretty fed-up crowd, cranking halting unresponsive cars in ponds of water. My no 8 started all right, and most of the others eventually. All our tyres burst though, and had to be changed – everything that only happens occasionally, happened. By 9 we got off and started over a worse road than I had dreamed one would ever drive a car over. Water filled the holes, and it was impossible to guess a puddle from a pit. We bumped along fairly gaily for a bit – through Salini – until we came upon the lorries of last night, stuck in every position of defeat. Some had fallen off the road altogether, some were merely over their axles in the soft new mud. Our guide, a Russian Irishman, decided we had better leave the road at this point and cut across the grass hills – to do this we had to get up a bank of about 50 yards, the track churned up, and at an angle of about 50 degrees. Mud below so we could get no speed up. The kitchen got up part of the way and we all hauled her the rest. The mud was either half way up one's legs or too slippery to get any grip at all. My car came next, and so on, till we had them all safe up. After mine they came by a different track and got on better. The rain hardly stopped all day and we were frozen and so hungry. The cars stuck by turns all the way. The lorries specially had a bad time.

After 9 hours we achieved our 15 miles. It was a huge relief to get on the road again. The Greys had arrived two days before and we had pictured warm dry beds and lots and lots of food ready for us. We found - the Greys preparing the huge barracks for 200 wounded next day. The <u>whole</u> place was full of yelling orderlies splashing whitewash recklessly over walls, floor, and ceiling – <u>and</u> us. Food was none - water – none - I could have howled – if there had not been 75 people in our one room – and my bed had to be found – unpacked – and set up – then a wash, and a ship's biscuit with some tongue on it, and tea.

3. At work at last

3. At work at last.

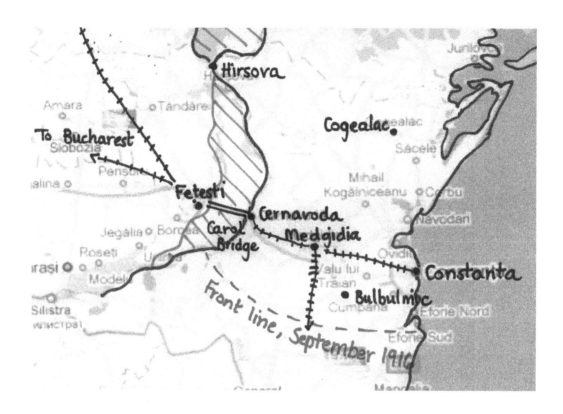

Medgidia: Dr Inglis' hospital was here, 4 – 21 October
Bulbul Mic: The Transport was stationed at Bulbul Mic with the S.W.H. Field Hospital, run by Dr Chesney, 9 – 20 October.

Distances: Medgidia to Cernavoda: 15 miles
Medjidia to Bulbul Mic: 15 miles
Bulbul Mic to the front line: 5 - 7 miles

The hospital in Medgidia was a former barracks, two-storey, and set on a hill overlooking the Cernavoda - Constanta railway. Two hundred yards away was the second-century Trajan's Wall, and the road to the front ran past. The ground floor was converted to two 100-bed wards, with the side rooms becoming the theatre and theatre dressing-room. At first the women slept upstairs in the former granary, but as soon as the tents were pitched then that too was made ready for patients. The hospital's main inconvenience was that there was no running water; it had to be fetched from a pump up on the hill, or from the Russian hospital next door, and then boiled on a small Ludgate boiler.

A second hospital was set up at Bulbul Mic, fifteen miles further on, and some five to seven miles from the front line.

Field road from Bulbul Mic to the front – shells ahead.

Wednesday 4th October

In the morning the cars were ordered out at 10, and we set off for our first attempt to Bulbul Mic. This far there was a hard highroad – a small village where we were told 1,000 wounded were lying together. A very nice Russian doctor came out of his tent dressing station and gave us orders. The lorry and five ambulances stayed there to ply all day between the village and our hospital. Mrs Haverfield in Onslow's car and a guide took me and three others on, up to the front. The road became a track of endless mud and mudholes, mud that would have wrenched any other cars' insides out. It was very ticklish driving. The cars boiled and had to be cooled from time to time. In front of us was a line along the horizon with guns. We struggled on over impossible tracks, with endless streams of carts, horse ambulances, soldiers returning for rest, groups of less seriously wounded walking back as best they could – all with gleaming white bandages, a striking contrast to their dull, drab clothes caked with mud. A dead horse and a dead dog, and then a wrecked village without a house with a roof on it. Here we stopped at the dressing tent and took in our cases. I daren't think of the mud holes and the nightmare road. My car was the first to be loaded, two stretcher cases, one head case – delirious – and another with a fractured thigh. It was for them the horror, and I, to lighten it as far as possible and so I drove them back and the memory of it will always be there till I die.

I had Reay as my orderly and she behaved better than I did – once we had the car pointed back, there were a dozen tracks, all of which R. was equally certain was the right one. We had come the wrong way – so could not settle it by following our own tracks. The plain – and all these tracks – and not to know the shortest way home – with the wounded screaming at every jolt. A dozen times I had to turn R. off to lighten the car before we came to holes, and I made her walk miles across a field too soft for even a plucky little Ford. We stuck once and had to wait till a group of men going up pushed us out. Once lost, every landmark becomes horribly disfigured, and distorted, and we were lost. We had not learned how to pronounce Medgidia, so utterly bewildered all of whom we asked the way. The last straw was the track up to Bulbul Mic, so churned up that one could not hope to get through, but had to skid along the sloping bank by the side.

At Bulbul Mic my orderly and I were so anxious about the head case we asked the doctor to look at him. He told us to drive on. The relief of getting on to the road! I think then my man fell asleep, and I believe I did too. We got back before dark and I found some of the others who had been between Bulbul Mic all day were going again, and so I left my orderly behind and came on to Bulbul Mic. The doctor sent us with loads to the station. Here we found no accomodation – crowds huddled together on the stone floor of the station room, and a group round a fire in the yard. We set out to get straw and spent ages making straw beds for all, then feeling we could do nothing more, we laid them down and left them – alone except for a man who might have been a doctor, or a stationmaster, for all the interest he took.

Back to Bulbul Mic, where we took two more, and then home, where we arrived about midnight. So we spent our first day at our work.

Thursday 5th October

Up at 3.45 and back to Bulbul Mic to fetch and carry from there on, all day and so on. We were only able to take eighty in, and so had to take them to other hospitals. I took walking wounded to no. 5 station, where they took them in – jolted them off their stretchers and then brought them back to me. This happened again – a Russian system no doubt. I returned to Bulbul Mic after finally placing my wounded and was there given two special cases to take to Abequor. One of the doctors came too. He was quite sharp with one of the officers when he complained. I went at the slowest possible pace, which he thought more comfortable, though I should have thought it better to get it over a little sooner. We crawled there at a foot's pace, and my car boiled all the way. The doctor at Abequor begged me to take some of their wounded to Medgidia. They had nothing but horse ambulances. The men were lying on stretchers outside the crowded huts. I plied between there and Medgidia till 4 when I was wanted back at Bulbul Mic as my friend was expecting a fresh lot in during the afternoon. They came. The doctor took us down to into their mess and gave us supper there. They fed like princes and we were all ravenous. After supper we took more wounded to the station, where they now have a tent for them. We took in our last at Bubul Mairie before midnight again – and got home at 1 am. Carrying the men in I felt giddy, and odd, but they did not feel the least heavy.

Called at 4 am – Breakfast was not to be had before we started so we just took ship's biscuits and set off for another day. We were cold – stiff – and were cross about getting no hot tea. As usual we slept in our clothes and went out without attempting to wash. My car started up beautifully and we were away in good time. My friend greeted us with surprise and asked how it was done – "Do not English girls need to sleep, as others do?" I said they did, dreadfully. The orders were to go up to the front again. I left Reay at Bulbul Mic, as she is only a make weight. Mackenzie came up as I was getting off, and we went together. The road had dried up a great deal and we got on to Abequor without any sticks or boils. At Abequor they were eagerly awaiting us as the dressing tent was overflowing into the yard. Many lighter cases were left outside. Jensen came up with the touring car and took seven of these straight back to Medgidia station.

My cases were all Russians. I took two stretchers and one sitting case by me – I chose an arm case that could get out if necessary – and we all set off on the track home with our thirteen. It was an easy matter this time and we came on steadily till we got to Bulbul Mic village. Just before the field road ends is the worst bit of all. At Bulbul Mic I left only my worst case, picked up an orderly, and took the others to our hospital. Some of the ambuli were not out, so Hodges was on stretcher duty and we carried the men in together. I hate doing it as they are too heavy for us all, and though one would not drop the stretcher, one might fall under it.

Back again to Bulbul Mic – till 10 pm, when I knocked off, as I had had enough, and wanted to sleep. Never slept a wink all night, all the same. The guns stopped yesterday morning, so once we can get this lot cleared we can sleep. The lorries were out for sitting cases all day.

Saturday 7th October

The car stood three days and nights of this and then developed a very definite and grisly knock. I took her down completely with the help of the doctor's shover[1] and we thought it was the camshaft, but could find nothing sufficient to explain the racket, so put her up again and I drove her to Chernavoda. The doctor's Polish shover came too. The highroad had dried up and so we had not to go across the hills. We arrived, about 3, and I sat and wrote letters in the car in the yard till M. Marcel condescended to look at her. He promised to attend to her next day and when he had time, to show me where I could sleep. A Romanian officer came in, with his car, and whiled away an hour talking to me. I explained laboriously in my best French, in answer to his questions, that we were not suffragettes, that we had no destructive instincts and that Serbia had sent to England to ask for us. Also that we cut our hair not to look like men, but to avoid bugs. I think he understood some of it. At 8 Marcel said he could not put me up, as I had hoped, but said one of his mechanics, an Italian, would house me. My soldier friend took us there. The Italian I found lived by himself in a two room house. In one of the rooms with the bed, I slept, and he roughed it in the other. Supper was rather a tragedy. First came olives in oil, then meat, too tough to eat, with salad. He crowded it onto my plate and I ate though it was horrid. While he ate with many Noms de Dieu, he explained that it was paraffin he had used. I had struggled on with it. Then we had burnt bread – and tea. I went to bed feeling sick and hungry. All night I coughed, and all night I was gnawed to the bone. Whenever I coughed particularly, the mechanic came in to ask after me. An oddish night if ever.

Sunday 8th October

My host was up early. I followed down to the workshop at 9, and found Marcel awaiting to take me a trial run. By 11 I had got all the jobs done and the Pole turned up, so I drove home. No 8 had not given up knocking, but went perfectly.

---

[1]   At the Opera, the Grand Duchess had asked Jensen if she was a "shouver" (chauffeur) and the Transport gleefully applied the name to themselves and other drivers thereafter. Given the amount of time they spent shoving cars out of the mud, it seemed fitting.

Found the Buffs on the verge of going into camp and spent the day there sorting things out. Orders were to take nothing. Some of the Greys were to go and form a dressing station, with Dr Chesney in charge,[1] and all the Buffs but two – I took two in my car, but had a puncture on the way. Mrs Haverfield overtook me in the ambulance and insisted on stopping to help me to help me put on the Stepney and sent the others on. It was not a success. The car began to make a quite new noise and I got strafed all the way here.

Camp when we arrived looked very attractive, but too huge. Mrs Haverfield had the mess tent down in a minute, and four of the tents, putting 3 in each. I somehow kept one to myself.

Putting up tents: Donisthorpe, Cunningham, Maguire, Ellis, Plimsoll, and Reaney

---

[1] The B Hospital remained as a separate unit. It consisted of twelve people: Dr Chesney, medical student Rendel, administrator Miss Henderson, Matron Vizard, nurses Bangham, Jenkins, and Jackson, cook Ford and orerlies Moir, Grant, Fawcett and Turner. It was beside a Serbian Field Hospital run by Dr Stanojevik. The women had the assistance of Serbian orderlies.

Job done: Cunningham, Plimsoll, Maguire, MacDougall. (Below) The kitchen car.

60

In camp: Hedges, Carlyon, Mrs Haverfield and Donisthorpe.

Lovely weather, and endless flat grassland stretched away to the front. Bulbul Mic with the station on one side. Slept so happily by myself, for the first time since I left England.

Peaceful days. No sound of guns, and, but for the ceaseless streams of troops marching up, and the rumble of army carts along the distant road, it were hard to believe in the war.

Some officers brought horses and we rode them. It was delightful to ride away over the country. Though the ground was as hard as a brick and the horses fat and puffing, I loved it.

Tuesday 12th October

Another hot day, and still no sound of guns. An enemy aeroplane came over and was fired at pretty wildly, without result. Livesay and Monfries returned from Constantia – they had a pretty rough time. The town was bombarded by nine aeroplanes and the streets were littered with dead and dying. They came back pretty defeated. However they have secured a real live mechanic[1] to help us out. An immense relief to most of us.

I went a long quiet ride on Monjie – the horse of my friend Nicolai – and then Mrs Haverfield, Murphy, Glubb, Carlyon and I went to tea at the Russian mess in Bulbul Mic. I got in from my ride after they had started, but found Nicolai waiting for me. We arrived there ages first and sat in the garden till the others came. Then came a wonderful meal – sausage, bread, butter, the first we had seen for weeks, biscuits, jam, crème de menthe, two kinds of wine, and chocolate and cigarettes all the time. I talked hard to Nicolai in German - Murphy in English to her neighbours who spoke only in Russian. Carlyon sat silent between Glubb and I, and drank crème de menthe at about hundred miles an hour while Glubb whispered to a big man at the foot of the table. Mrs H also was rather good at it. Anyway, Nicolai promised to take me to the front on horses one Sunday. Long after dark we were there. A mandolin and guitar were produced, and they played most beautifully.

While we were there some troops marched past the window singing, as Russians love to do. Their singing brings tears to the eyes but one would fight for them till one died – they sing as
they go into battle.

Going riding:

Jensen and Nicolai

---

[1]   The real live mechanic was George, a Romanian refugee from Constanta who attached himself to the Transport. He was a motor-mechanic by trade, and Hodges later said that during the retreat he really saved the Unit from being taken prisoner or shelled to pieces.

Saturday 14th October

Had my first real taste of war first hand. Three doctors came for a car and I was sent. We had not got to _____ before we heard bombs. There we found three planes bombing the barracks and all the soldiers lying out in the fields on their faces. We rushed through to Medgidia. There was a bombardment going on there too. As we passed the Red Cross food place, a man was hit, blown to bits. On to the station. There a mass of carts were rushing out into the open – one cart was hit, the horses terribly hurt, one died at once. My passenger nearly wrecked us by dropping his hand over my legs. It was hard work!

On into the plain. Here everyone had rushed for safety. We drove on, right away to the town we were going to - about six miles - then returned. Just as we reached the aerodrome, we realized that that was the chief object of attack. Bombs were falling in the lower part of the town. My passenger said 'Turn and drive as hard as you can.' Quite useless, as bombs were falling all around, behind and before. I then discovered I had a tyre down, and shoved on my Stepney. Meanwhile my passengers had jumped out of the car and taken cover under a thistle. I would have too had I thought anything made any difference. After what seemed hours they moved off and we drove on by a different road to avoid the horrors of the station. We stopped at the café and he left me to help at the hospital. After I had been there about half an hour everyone suddenly rushed for their houses and I realised they were at it again. I far preferred the street but was shoved into the café but could not bear the idea of the roof over my head so went and sat on the step of my beloved Royce. I had plenty of time as I sat there to take in the horrors of the streets. They had been pretty well cleared of the victims of the last raid, and not a soul was to be seen. A cat stole past me, carrying in its mouth the thumb of a man. After a bit, one of the officers came out of the mess opposite and invited me in. I explained that I could not face a roof as well as a bomb on my head – that I dare not. 'I also am a coward, mademoiselle,' he said, and came and sat with me in the ambulance and held my hand, rather tight – to my great comfort.[1] The next areoplane to drop things dropped some little parcels that looked like sweets within three yards of us. He said they were poisoned. When I got up to crank the car, I found I had stopped her in a pool of blood.[2]

My passengers came back at last, and I drove home. About ten dead lying on the road. Just as I arrived an aeroplane came over our camp, stopped and dropped a bomb, fairly wide.

In the evening I rode – alone, thank goodness! The others were all called out later for wounded, from all parts. Many were killed. As an officer said, 'Mais que voulez vous – c'est la guerre.'

Through noise, or cat, very sick all night.

---

[1] The preceding six sentences were not in the diary, but were typed into the typescript.

Sunday 15th October

All cars out for wounded. All the neighbouring villages sent in for cars. I was out with some doctors all day. Fearfully hot.

Russian officers came up with horses in the evening. I felt too utterly ill to ride. Most of the camp are crawling about poisoned by flies or our beastly food.

They all re-appeared as we were sitting round our campfire after supper and sang and danced. They brought some soldiers to do peasant dances – Nicolai sat by me, but I was too chilled to be amused.

Monday 16th October

Found Tindall rather cry-y by her car and said hopefully, 'Let me try, I expect she'll start.' Tindall's reply of 'Yes, I fear she will' was nothing if not honest.

About eight now have dysentry – I too – but not bad enough for bed. Not many calls for cars now, for the last four days, just as well.

Much better, shifted wounded further back. Aeroplanes over again, and more bombs dropped near camp. Russian and Serbian uniforms swarm here. Feeling pretty ill.

Out all day till 4, bomb cases. Some women and one child. Nicolai came for me at about 4.30 and we rode off to the front. I rode a funny little rather fumbling horse called Kopjic. We rode first to Abequor, the village we had got wounded from the first day. Here we asked for Nicolai's friends who were to go out with us. We could not find them, so rode on through another village where horses were looking out of the windows of the houses – and where the only house with a roof was a dressing station. It seemed odd that they should prefer these ruins for a camp, rather than the open country, but I suppose the walls provided some shelter. The ghosts of hearths would have driven me out. Little groups were crouching over fires, cooking among the debris.

We passed some open country, up a slope, past trenches and barbed wire entanglements and past a little knot of men. As we were reaching the top of the rise we met an officer coming back who told us we were almost up to the last outpost and were wandering over to the Bulgar lines. We returned with him to where we ought to have left our horses. He left us, after giving us a man as guide. We followed him along past pickets, hidden guns, over trenches, until at last we found the man we were looking for, the head of all the artillery in the Drobruja.

It was dark by now, and as we looked into the distance it was most picturesque. The great man was dictating letters in a dugout, to a Serb, or someone. We walked along till we could get down, and then by the trench to his 'house'. Here I had a good chance to take it all in, while he finished his letters. About 8 x 8 feet wide covered with tarpaulin – and also the floor. It looked a comfortable enough little home to me after a damp flapping tent. For furniture , a bare table, 4 chairs, a stove - and that was all, except in a corner a guitar. From a nail in the wall hung his belt and sword. His letters finished, we all came and talked, in French and also German, and they broke into Russian. I had not to explain my existence or the object of our coming, as they already knew about us (the old man had seen our cars at Abequor) and approved. Then he played his guitar and sang Russian songs, while Nicholai and the others joined in, clanking their spurs to the rhythm. Outside soldiers passed in the dark, or stopped and saluted at the door, with endless messages.

Supper came soon, with the now old familiar apology, 'A la guerre – comme à la guerre.' Meat and macaroni for each of us four, and knives and forks for two, liqueurs, which I agitated them terribly by not drinking tumblers of – then white bread and mugs of milk. I had seen neither for weeks. More songs and cigarettes till coffee came. The dear old man was charming. He said I was the first woman to visit him, as their ladies were not allowed to go up really, but I, who was doing the work of a man, should have the privileges of both. His little tent was lined with felt and also looked solidly comfortable. He explained that he had to leave it for his dugout at daybreak, every morning, because of the fire. We left amid handshaking and promises to return again one day. I somehow feel we should not meet again there though. One of the others accompanied us to where we left our horses. It was pitch dark. Here we all got on and rode to Abequor. The road was very rough indeed. At Abequor, Nicolai's friend stopped to leave his greatcoat and Nicolai found more friends. They begged us to come in, but I was very firm – it was already late and once off one's horse it usually means a meal and at least one hour before one is allowed to leave. After seeing us well on our way the man left us. The road was atrocious so I was not at all surprised when my horse fell head over heels, and shot me onto my head. Poor Nicolai was horrified – and showed it – so like a foreigner. After that episode he flatly refused to go at a whack. It was eerie riding over those plains without a road, and not enough light to see one's horse's ears. We talked German to each other except when he lost his head and burst into Russian, and I had to tell him what I thought of him in English.

At about 10.30 we came upon the camp rather suddenly and I was a good deal sorry my adventure was over. Reported myself and went to bed, to find I was rather tired, and ill.

Two days in bed – dysentry, curse it. Chesney absolutely refused to let me move.

Guns, as never before, ceaseless, ceaseless guns. Woke to hear them in the night and could not sleep again. All cars were in readiness, for it was too obvious that a big attack was in progress. The attack grew near that we had prayed might be delayed till we were further reinforced by Russians. Our little Serb infantry and Russian artillery. I gave my car over to

Gartlan – nobody else has touched her but me before, but I know I could not do a day's work. Then as I lay and listened I heard bombs falling around and could hear car after car going out. Then the hideous sound of an aeroplane overhead, and Hedges came to tell me there were three flying around, up to no good. <u>Then</u> came the bombs. I got up just as one fell in our camp between the cars and the Greys – one of the Greys was hit in the arm. I was jerked back onto my bed by the concussion. Three fell together in the space on the right, killing three men. I always wonder they don't make a job of it and wipe us and the village with its camp out altogether. Nineteen were killed in the village and twenty-seven wounded. The order came to decamp, just as I was dressed, and we, the sick and all that were left, fell to - packing up our goods and taking down the tents. In a while orders came from Inglis that all sick whether they liked it or not were to go to Medgidia. Mrs Haverfield of course expected us all to say we weren't sick, but I knew I was, and went with eight others. Needless to say this happens just when drivers are most needed. Onslow drove us in, eight of us. We arrived in utter depression at A camp to find no tent up, and nowhere to go. I sat in the kitchen tent for three hours and snoozed till the tent was up, then I went and put up my bed and got into it. Nothing was done for anyone and we spent a day and night in supreme discomfort. Meanwhile wounded were pouring into our hospital - the transport were out all night, I think.

Douglas Gordon Baxter, 1991:

Her motive for taking part - which could at the time have involved other loftier ideals including that much decried 'last refuge' - may not have taken the form she was to give it later, which, expressed, turned out to be that times of great crisis found people divided into two groups, those who needed help, the helpless, and those who could give help, the helpers, and she was a helper. It was about all she ever did say, as to the why, of her own participation in those events. After this time the idea of killing anything, anyone, was always abhorrent to her. 'Beastly' said very vehemently, was the word usually used to condemn, not only killing, but individual acts of aggression falling far short of that. When this awareness that not killing was better, on the whole, than killing, gradually dawned, must in large part go down to her Russian experience. Before then, field sports had been a prominent feature of her life, but after that, a steady decline, if that's the word, set in, until she no longer took part in any of it, and had she the faith in societies that set themselves up to regulate the actions of others in such things would surely have been a founder member, but, as it was, not having that faith and believing that setting a personal example was all, turned herself into a crusade for 'those persons' who lived where it mattered most to her, at Caolas Mor. Then, much earlier, her exposure to Buddhism must have left its mark, perhaps lay dormant, but was resurrected later in a veneration for life in its minute, least-regarded forms.

Marsali Taylor, 2011:

I remember the goldfinches that flew in and out of her kitchen window at Caolas Mor. I remember the two herring gulls that she fed, Nakker and Poodle. She had an otter for a time, too; she found it in a trap with its leg broken, and took *Mine* over to fetch the doctor to set it, there being no vet for miles. With her eye on him, he came, and Oscar mended and went back into the wild.

One of her vivid, meticulous fungi paintings has hung on my wall for over thirty years, in Dundee, in Edinburgh and now in Shetland, a ring of different species, with the lean, ragged whitecaps at the back, curving round to the amber of the deadly Fly agaric. A piece was torn out of it before I got it, but I have not the skill to resurrect the missing triangle.

4. The retreat to Galatz: 22nd- 24th October

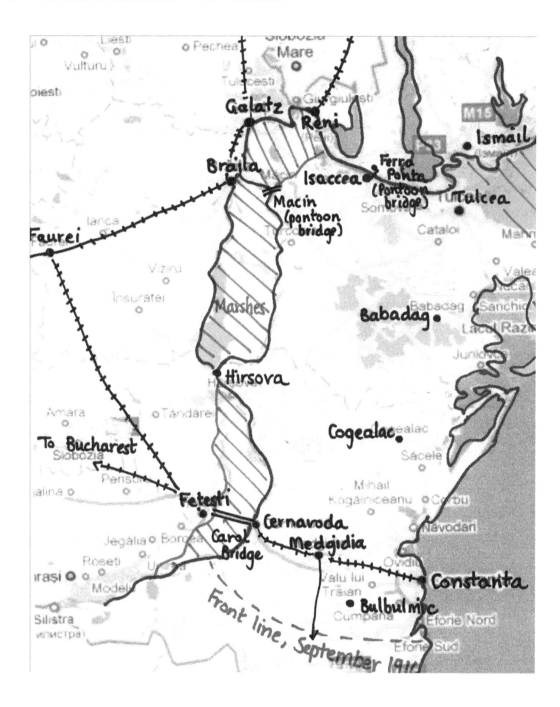

From Medjidia to Cernavoda was 15 miles; Cernavoda to Galatz was about 90 miles by water, and more than double that by train.

On Saturday 14th October there had been an aeroplane bombardment on Medgidia. Several of the S.W.H women had close escapes; Bell, who was soon to have a nervous breakdown, was at the station and behaved with cool courage, pacifying frightened people and holding terrified horses, according to Milne, who was with her.

News came only in snatches to the units. They could see the gunfire and streams of troops, but heard only vague rumours - the Russians had gone to reinforce their own army, the Romanians gave way, the Bulgars had broken through, the Carol Bridge was taken. In fact they were in great danger; the Allied lines had broken, and the Germans and Bulgarians had captured towns within a fifteen-mile radius of Bulbul Mic: Tuzla, on 20th October, Cobadinu and Toprasari on the 21st. The oil tanks of Constanta were burning on the 22nd. Medgidia and Constanta were taken on the 23rd and Cernavoda on the 24th.

Almost all of the S.W.H equipment was sent off to Galatz by train, under the care of two orderlies, and the personnel of the main hospital followed, by train, in cars or on the back of a lorry. The sick, including Birkbeck, were also sent by train, through Cernavoda, Fetesti, Faurei and Braila. The field hospital was maintained until the last minute, and those women were evacuated with the Serbian Field Hospital, going cross-country to Galatz on ox-carts. The Transport were still taking wounded men to the last.

Separated in the chaos and panic of a full-scale retreat, and unable to communicate with anyone else, each little party had to make its own decisions. Intelligence and determination saw each group through safely, along with almost all of their equipment.

It was to be almost two weeks before they all assembled at Galatz, shocked and horrified by the scenes of panic they had witnessed.

Sunday 22nd October

Awake all night. At about 9.30 – bombs! – nearer, till we heard again the aeroplanes getting louder and louder. Those who were energetic enough went out and described to us their evolutions. They were out for the aerodrome and station, I suppose, but were very near us. During the morning all but I and two others got up and left the discomfort of our tent - we preferred anything to being moved. Ten days starving has taken most of the zipp out of me and feeling too weak to be heroic.

Guns distinctly nearer all day. Bulbul Mic is in the 3rd line and beyond that there isu nothing to stop them. We hear the Transport have been sent back from Constanta, though not ours, we think. It's on a level with Bulbul Mic, so I wonder why they are busy between both lines. We must be retreating steadily. Many rumours come up to us. Towards evening we heard the others had evacuated soon after we left, to this village halfway. They were out all night bringing in wounded. The last line was being held, and at night they were sent back here. Wounded pouring in, but only dressed and sent on.

Guns, guns, guns – ceaseless streams of carts – refugees all day – and herds of cattle being driven over the hills.

B dressing station had over two hundred from that night alone.

Bell left tonight. I'd have gone with her, if I had not been ill, just had to see her go off to heaven knows where - gave her all the money I had and wished her best.[1]

More rumours – that the road to Caracin and also to Chernavoda cut off, we in full retreat and the order to evacuate the hospital. All stores to be sent to Chernavoda – the doctor came round and let all except Hedges and me get up and work. Got up and packed and dressed but went back into my bed till final orders. Chernavoda with its bridge and also this place Medgidia on account of its railway are of great importance.

Where are our friends – where is Nicolai?

Hedges and I lay in the middle of our possessions, while the others packed - and left – given a ship's biscuit each as well as milk and Allenburys.[2] Then the order came to pack. We then packed our beds, and lay on the ground till further orders. They came soon enough, and the

---

[1] Bell was the only one of the S.W.H women to suffer a breakdown. She was recently widowed, having seen her husband killed by a tiger just a few months previously. Miss Henderson, the administrator, had gone with Bell to Constanta, and seen her on a train to Bucharest, returning to Medgidia just before Constanta fell to the Bulgarians. This paragraph, and all further mentions of Bell, do not appear in the typescript.

[2] Allenbury's Medicated Throat Pastilles, containing menthol, cocaine, red gum, eucalyptus, guacicum, rhatany, potash, borax, formaldehyde and cinnamon oil.

tent came down on us as we were clearing it. Then to the hospital, where we lay on the now empty beds in the wards - I took the trouble to disinfect mine first. Orders to evacuate the hospital came during the afternoon and this was done. Meanwhile the Transport disappeared – which left the whole work to Clibborn. The last to go was a seriously wounded officer. His stretcher was put down near my bed to await the ambulance. The concern of his soldier servant was one of the most pathetic things I have seen - squatting on the floor by his master, hugging his sword, and never taking his eyes from him for a moment, but to go again and again to the door to see if the car had returned. They were a pathetic little group, with the sister-in-charge with her lantern, and I breathed more freely when at last they trooped out. He will die, they say, but who knows? All night the orderlies packed. They are beyond wonder. And all night the guns grew nearer, or seemed to.

At 4 am we heard a rumour that we were to be off at 6; at 5.30, that the Bulgarian retreat had been checked, and that we were to prepare the hospital for more wounded. Some said they'd go to church, and others made other peaceful plans. At 12 we heard we had half an hour. Up and driven to the station by Clibborn – Matron, who's pretty bad with dysentry, on a stretcher, and Hedges and I. S. had been down town – most of the shops were shut and there were few windows with glass left in them. The road was fairly packed with refugees, but most had already gone. It was with almost too much sorrow that we left – wounded were all along the road – but what could we do? All the other hospitals were evacuating also, and we had our orders. At the station was a rather disconsolate scene - our Greys, having absorbed every rumour, the most striking of which had been that the R. I. train we were to have left on had left. This for once proved true, and we were refugees indeed on our bed bundles, in torrents of rain, while the leaders argued. It was interesting and tragic to see the refugees huddled in open trucks, piled high with pathetic treasure. One dear old woman sheltered a puppy under her shawl, and from the cloak of another, two long-necked geese peered. The saddest of all were the children, who knew only the physical discomfort of the moment. Food has been impossible to get.

Refugees, Megidia station

Finally after six, a troop train came in; we were shoved into a cattle truck, all baggage that had not already been seen off (our rugs rolls) was thrown in and then we heard we might have one second class carriage too. Some had to stay in the horse truck with the luggage and twelve Serbian soldiers. I, Little, Vizard and Lewis[1] stayed. We meant to have one side for ourselves, and let the twelve Serbian soldiers have the other. Cris[2] at once began to clear the place out. However a terribly wounded man crawled to the door, and I hauled him in – others followed, and before we realised it we had fourteen pretty bad cases, and no means of attending to them. However, better with us than in the open trucks without food. Cris set to, and we made each a bed of rug rolls as they came in, laying them down like sandwiches. Then we gave bread all round, before attempting to attend to their wounds, most of which had not even first dressings.

The last to join us were an officer and a young doctor. I tried to eject the latter as we had no use of sound men in our midst. However Cris said he was of use and might come. At 4 we left. We heard first that the Bulgars were in Bulbul Mic. However more and more troops were pouring into Medgidia and we had great hopes of them, for all a retreat in the rain is rather a hopeless prospect. The evening we spent padding the wounds that had already been dressed, and had come undone, and in dressing the others as best we could – many wounds had maggots. That really amounted to using what little dressing we had and using one's clean handkerchiefs as bandages – for slings we used everything from Little's belt to the cord from my sleeping bag. They slept very soon - I had a tin of cocoa, and we boiled some water over what remained of my Symphalite stove – the cooker part, I held the kettle over it until at last it boiled. Then cocoa all round, and they slept. Extraordinarily soon they slept, but were suffering from hunger and exhaustion. Someone had a lamp, and this we hung from the roof. Having done all we could, we ourselves settled down where we could in the middle. We had four upright canvas chairs. I, with the little doctor on one side and an old Red Cross Ruskie wounded on the other, sat with chairs touching - our feet on a bale covered with my sheepskin.[3] The others lay on heaps of rugs. Bombs fell about at intervals. One especially made me jump out of my skin - the train came to an abrupt stop. Starvation diet <u>does</u> make one jumpy and except for my one famous meal in the dugout I had eaten nothing but milk and two biscuits for ten days. Tonight however I had cocoa and some black bread, so the shortage of food did not bother me.

Again and again and again we stopped - once for ages when an officer came and said we could go no further, we were cut off. This was in the middle of a marsh and we heard guns very near and saw red flashes. However we did go on, past what appeared to be a burning village. Dense columns of smoke were blowing the other way. Appearing in the smoke moved along stores and guns and soldiers. We wondered who, and where they were going next. They were going the way we had come from.

---

[1] Vizard was Matron; Little and Lewis were nurses.

[2] Cris was their Serbian orderly and interpreter – he seemed to be the only Serb soldier who spoke English (the common language was generally German). He was tall, guant and harassed.

[3] This and the preceding sentence were torn out of the typescript.

Now the rug around us lay next to the shoulder of my Ruskie brother, and, as he said, 'You will get fleas and other things, worse than me' - so I reluctantly got up and spent the rest of the night on the floor with the S. cook, and in talking to Little. From his chair the doctor told us what he thought of English women and gave us both his advice. Too utterly stone weary to resent. Little was enjoying it immensely. He was <u>that</u> provoking.[1]

Nights vary in length but this, though light at six, was <u>the</u> very longest I ever lived through - All night, more or less, one of the wounded was awake, and others groaned while they slept. At 2 we were roused at a stop by someone knocking on the door. It was the illest looking man I ever saw. As I hauled him in, I knew. He came in - like a man with the plague. The doctor asked him in Russian, and he confessed to cholera. Out into the rain he pushed him, and left him – alone - I threw a blanket after him - and then the dark.

Cernavoda, at about 9.30 having taken fifteen hours to travel as many miles. Here Monfries and I got out to buy bread, or steal it. The town was deserted and glass from every window was smashed. We did not go down but, by the bridge, marched into what appeared to be the headquarters of the military. Two officers were quite interested, and gave us two loaves of bread. We were wondering whether we should go for a walk for an hour when we heard the everlasting bombs - the train got away at once, and we had to run for it. I landed in a horse truck on my face. Monfries fell and got left. As we rushed for the bridge they were trying for it, and I was more afraid than ever in my life - they hit it, but behind us. Meanwhile - as Monfries described when she rejoined us by the next train after it had been mended (slight damaged only), everyone bolted for their funk holes and she into an empty train, the glass of which was all blown out. We were missed by very little, and it was a specially nasty occasion. High bridge over big river. Once over the Danube we all felt as safe as houses. When we got bombed twice further on we took it quite nicely.

At Fetesti a huge great official roared at me to follow. He turned into a frightfully nice doctor on a Red Cross train who took me inside, gave me chocolate, introduced me to some lovely Red Cross sisters and finally sent me off with an orderly with a sack of packets of sterile dressings. The Romanians spotted it I think and followed, collecting like a snowball till I arrived back chez nous with about thirty. We fairly got to work and in a rough and ready way patched them up. Here, a boy led me to a cattle truck on my own train and introduced me to what was afterwards known as my ward. Here, lying on the floor on a heap of manure, were eleven stretcher cases lying on the floor. There was no question of dressing their wounds thoroughly in such filthy surroundings. It would have been folly to uncover anything, so we just packed those that had been dressed, fixed up slings and roughly washed all that we could who had not been touched.

---

[1] The first sentence of this paragraph seemed unreadable to the typist, as a gap was left, and the final three sentences were torn out of the typescript.

None were fit to move, and we had nowhere to put them. We decided it was better not to disturb the floor, and so left it. I got them hot tea and bread. Little as interpreter came and said they had had none since Medgidia. At the next stop I got Dr Corbett to come and see them, and she gave me blankets for them, and we left them as comfortable as we could. I shifted into the second class carriage for a bit and slept. We heard we had to change and the other cars would go on to Bukarest. Dr Corbett said Cliver[1] and I might go on with the train and do what we could for the wounded. We packed our haversacks and were all ready. At 10 we got to _____ and heard we had not to change after all - so all went on together.[2]

I prowled along the train in the dark and up to the horse truck with a kettle of hot tea. They were all awake and terribly cold, but went to sleep before I left them. I think the hot tea made them sleep. The most uncomfortable one had boots - wet - over flannel bandages. I found he had more flannel so pulled his boots off, rubbed his feet warm, put on the new dry bandages, emptied the manure out of his boots and replaced them, filled this time with the cleanest straw I could find. He too fell asleep. Meanwhile the train wandered on. One man in the truck was suffering evidently from shell-shock. He moved restlessly around the crowded truck in delirium. Every now and then he screamed, and talked and shouted all the time. I got Little in at a stop. He got worse, and we soon saw he was quite raving mad. The difficulty was to keep him from stumbling over the bodies of the other men on the floor. One man with a fractured thigh suffered terribly, and at every jolt he too screamed. A man shot through the face cried quietly all night. Our candle was two inches only and we had a quarter of a box of matches with which we were as sparing as we could be. When necessary we struck a match but dare not light our candle, for it had to last till dawn. A man with an abdomen wound coughed and died. The shell-shocked man got more and more noisy and so the night wore on. The only light in the truck between our matches were our luminous watches. I liked the gleam off Little's. At last we lit the candle having only two matches left. The shell-shocked man was being terribly sick now and getting more violent.

The candle burned lower and lower – Little and I began to talk rather feverishly about - other things - when the shell-shocked man jumped up, and as the candle gave its last flicker, he crumpled up - dead.

All the time the man with the head wound slept.

One seems to be always watching the sun rise these days.

---

[1] Cliver was one of the trained nurses.
[2] This paragraph from 'Little as interpreter' was removed from the typescript.

B. Track of wounded.

In Lewis's truck I found them pretty tucked up but their wounded pretty comfortable - those that still lived. A lot more had been put in a truck next door under our care. Little and I got a huge kettle of tea for them too, and bread. At _____ Cris and I got a huge jorum of soup from a Russian troop train going up. It was delicious - there was enough for all to have some. The refugees on the open trucks howled and cried for my kettle as I carried it past to the wounded, and one hardly knew which to give it to. Little and I then found forty in a truck slightly wounded and were standing outside pouring tea into their mess tins when the train gave a jolt and got under way. I hopped up, and Little next door. It was so stupid not to be able to talk to them. We could just, a little, and felt quite good friends all the same.

I dropped off at the next stop with my trusty kettle to find we were at last at Galatz. We arrived at 1 - our flight ended pour le moment. Here we unloaded our wounded and gave them into the charge of wonderful boy scouts, who, we afterwards learned, entirely run Galatz. So ended the first part of our retreat.

The Berry[1] unit met us and put up a huge tent for us in their hospital grounds and fed us. They lent us a car and drove Dr Corbett about, to the consul and so forth.

Have had no news of the rest of our people.

Refugees on the quayside at Galatz.

[1] Two units of the Red Cross, attached to the newly-formed Second Serbian Division, were in Galatz, using a former school as a hospital. Dr James Berry, his wife, Dr Frances Berry, and Dr Clemow were in charge.

Douglas Gordon Baxter, 1991

The condition of the Diaries proclaim that they too had been at war, at the front, and in 'The Retreat', and that they had suffered every bit as much as their owner and those whose existence they describe. They are tattered and stained, and had been dropped in the mud, often, 'the endless Russian mud'. They have that unmistakable appearance that soaking imparts to pages of a book, long since dried out, they were probably frozen solid from time to time in the Russian winter and thawed out before a fire. The leaves are coming out of a binding just sufficiently strong for a student's peacetime notes. Decay has set in along the edges giving them a nibbled appearance, as of mice having been at work, and minute mildewed particles disintegrate and get left behind with every reading. There is an overall yellowing, splashed deeper often, across a page, as if from some liquid, Tea! could it be? Yes, strong scalding tea, a mug of it, held in one hand while unsteadily writing with the other, crouched over a night halt before a flickering wood fire in a clearing of pines. When there was no firelight or lamps, the diaries were introduced to the joy of candles, a commodity that Aunt Ysabel never liked to be short of throughout her life, and candle-grease too forms part of the matrix holding the whole together. Their exterior does much, were it needed, to give them an appearance of unimpeachable authenticity, while inside there is a compelling immediacy about them, for they were written in brief snatches, in pauses between one event, often horrific, and the next, often ludicrous. The wonder is they were written at all in the first months, at least, as days seemed to pass when even sleep had to be abandoned to dozing over a steering wheel, only to be jerked awake by a sickening lurch into a great pothole, or the screams of her wounded 'passengers'.

Marsali Taylor, 2011:

Once I got a proper look at them, the state of the diaries worried me. Here was a historic document which ought to be in a library, where it could be conserved. I wanted to keep a digital copy, though – and so the long process of scanning began. The thread of binding of Diary 1 was already broken, and many of the leaves could be scanned separately. Diary 2, in better condition, had to be spread open, with one page projecting from the edge of the scanner, then turned. I took a j-peg of each page, then, when I found a sketch or a page of photographs, a separate tif of each.

5. Breathing space in Galatz: 25th October - 27th November

5. Breathing space in Galatz: 25th October - 27th November

Dr Inglis and some others had stayed at Braila, assisting in the hospital there; by 3rd November, all the nursing staff of the Medgidia hospital had joined her. Dr Chesney set up the field hospital at Ismail, where what remained of the Serbian division were billeted. The Russian reinforcements checked the Bulgarian advance, and the Transport went back and forward across the Danube to bring the wounded to Braila, before being sent to Ismail with Dr Chesney.

Braila: Dr Inglis' unit was here, 28 October – 6 December.

Galatz: Transport quarters, 27 October – 30 November.   S.W.H. supplies and baggage kept here, and some personnel working in hospitals.

Distances: Braila to Galatz: 13 miles by rail.

Galatz to Reni: 15 miles by water.

Friday, 27ᵗʰ October

During the next three days they filtered through in small parties, all with thrilling stories of adventure.

By Friday October 27th we had news of the main body of Transport at Braila - a few cars (no 8 among them) came in on Thursday with Onslow, eight Greys, eighty men, and all except Dr Inglis and two with her. Dr Chesney's party were located. The latter were fleeing in carts, and Clibborn, we heard, had last been seen with a broken leg, maybe kicked by a horse in the rush. Public opinion was extremely fierce against Inglis. She held them all back and defied all authorities.[1]

Saturday, 28ᵗʰ October

Slept one short night in a house, Little Ellis and I, in rooms to ourselves, for the first time for two months. Life now seems a little irresolute. We live in two great red lined tents and, except when the cars are wanted for jobbing, potter about the town and look longingly at the comforts we cannot afford to buy. Miss Henderson who is in charge of cashing our cheques has run out.[2] We each managed a meal out at the Café Universal, however, where we sat in our war begrimed clothes and ate frothy cake and drank delicious coffee. The inhabitants regard us with utter bewilderment. We have none of us a thing but what we stand up in, and find the manicured nails of the Romanian officers very irritating – it's through them this wholesale retreat. The Russians cannot contain themselves on the subject - their wish is, now that the Romanians had joined the Germans, for then they would have hampered them, and not us. The Russian soldiers have a bitter contempt for them, and indeed, after the panic along the roads during the retreat one could hate them. The Transport brought stories that hardly bear repetition, of the wholesale loot and plunder of the retreating army - it was panic - and of individual cases of brutality. As they took their cars through the fleeing crowds they were beseiged by people who hung on to the already overloaded ambulances and implored to be taken up. One man seeing a car threw away a little baby and jumped on. They took the baby and its mother. Another worse case was of an officer who pulled a woman and her child off a peasant cart and kicked the man till he was forced to drive on - these too they crowded in. Another of their protegees was an old old woman who they found with a bundle and her dog, a refugee from Constanta, crying by the roadside, having given up all hope. Her horse had broken down. She offered her dog, a black demon, when she was landed safely at Braila. Then there were five women and countless children sitting helplessly on their cart with one of their four horses down, and quite incapable of righting things for

---

[1] This sentence was crossed out in the typescript.

[2] Money was a perennial problem. Difficulties with getting money from England meant that Miss Henderson had to use part of the personal money deposited with her for running costs of the hospital.

themselves. They were set on their way also. When we met later on, one saw on every face what we have since called "the mark of the Exodus." We have all agreed not to talk about it. It's no use soaking one's mind in horror especially if it's real, and we all have seen things we are trying to forget, but we never never shall.

We spent five nights in the tent during which the ground and our blankets got wetter every hour, as it rained so. We had no chance to dry them as our only fire was the camp kitchen outside. The last day there I was driven out into the rain to sit by the fire - the Doctor rescued us, or rather the British Consul. He offered us a room in his house. That day Dr Inglis kept me 2 ½ hours in my car waiting for her in the rain, and I really think everyone in the car could have killed her. The others somehow survived. Here we found a room, with a fire, and I think I was nearer crying hysterically than ever before.[1] However I went straight to bed as near the fire as I could with a temperature and thawed my bones out, after 4 luxurious days in bed. The luxury was imaginary, I think as I could not eat the food provided by the unit, and the tin milk that usually comes to one's rescue was not to be had, so I just lay and ached and groaned at the fourteen shrill voices and the cigarette smoke. The third day someone found some real milk, and I got on then. The others stopped messing in here too.

Varying rumours reached us all the week. Some said the advance had been checked but the retreating army never ceased to pour into the town while some of the inhabitants left it.

---

[1] The preceding three sentences were torn out of the typescript.

84

Some of our people left too, on November 2nd - Clibborn, Monfries and Grey Mackenzie went home, with an Englishman in the diplomatic service.

Saturday 4th November

Moved to the Watsons' house, a real proper bedroom with chintz curtains - only two others in the same room and no cooking, or eating.

Tuesday 14th November

Recovering from jaundice thanks to Mrs Berry, she made them get[1] a nurse, and cared for me - I rather think I should have died else.

Rather worried to hear several people have wired to the consul, asking what has become of the unit, so I suppose this retreat has been in all the papers, and that the wires never got through. I sent one the day I got here, three weeks ago.

Wednesday 15th November

Mrs Berry had a long talk about going home. I am quite prepared to if I really cannot eat the food, but I think I can, now I have got really well - and she is willing for me to have another try. Meanwhile we are not a cheerful party here. Glubb cries for three quarters of every night, and Livesay scraps with M.H.[2] next door, day and night. Why can't we get some regular work again?

---

[1] The rest of this sentence has been removed from the typescript.
[2] Miss Henderson, the administrator.

Visiting the invalid: Livesay and Birkbeck.

Glubb getting firewood.

Red Cross barges at the quay.

Dr Inglis has started up a hospital at Braila and the Transport and Dr Chesney are at Ismail, but have not much to do.

Bell turned up here. Glubb met her in the town and brought her to see me - with no skirt, a R. soldier's cap and a huge chrysanthemum in the little hole of her leather coat. She looked - all they have said. It's too sad to believe almost, and I spend all day stopping people talk about her. She talked quite normally when alone with me. She is living - anywhere. At 4 am she appeared at the window asking to be let in. I let her in but M.H.[1] had been roused and turned her out. At 6 she came again - the others fled into the next room, and we had a long quiet talk. I'm trying to get her to go home. She slipped out of the window and ran away before M.H. returned. The thought that she will return any moment of the day or night is not comforting. The others of course are terrified. Happily M.H. did not come in or I think Bell would have shot her - and she says the only thing she distinctly remembers missing for years is the tiger that killed her husband, so it was as well H. kept away.[2]

Bell, at Medgidia.

[1] This seems to be Mary Henderson, the administrator, who had taken Bell to Constanta at the start of the retreat, rather than Mrs Haverfield, whose imperious attitude caused friction with a number of her drivers.

[2] This paragraph was omitted from the typescript.

Extraordinarily little war news reaches us, and no one is even sure of it when it does come.

We hear that the entire Romanian and Russian army that were in the retreat have been exchanged for troops from the north. The Romanians were all reservists and it is hoped that the morale of the new lot will not be infected by their predecessors. Russian General _____ has taken over command and Romanian General _____ has lost his. Romanians and Russians all say that the retreat was, after the first, panic pure and simple, and as panic spread nothing could be done, and no attempt was made to hold the Bulgars. There was panic in the army and it spread to the people, and there was wholesale helpless panic everywhere. In individual cases one saw it, and it's a horrible thing to see on a face and in an army. Several old campaigners who had been with retreating armies before have said they had seen and dreamed of nothing like this. Cernavoda bridge was blown up by the Russians and rebuilt by the Germans. Two regiments were allowed to cross the Danube before the Romanians blew it up again. The two regiments were cut off in the marshes and massacred to a man. The opposing army here seems to be composed of a few Bulgars and Turks led and fortified by a very large percentage of Germans. I pray that if we get taken next time I may fall into the hands of a Turk. It's very cheering to hear we have some on our part of the line. Stories of German and Bulgar atrocities here rival those one heard of from Belgium in horror. The difference is only that here one is told all, while in England one was spared details unless one wished for them.

Saturday 18th November

The cold weather has certainly begun. A biting wind that cuts through everything and cuts slices off our cheeks, gives one the appetite of a wolf, and drives one out for walks in self-defence. I am out now and getting some energy and muscle back again.

I went for three joy rides in the car with Livesay, that made a great difference, and was great fun.

During the last month Galatz has changed a great deal. All the leaves are off the trees. The people are all dressed in furs and the officers appear in lovely coats of blue with fur collars to their ears. The ladies are smart and good looking but to us their too obvious make-up seems rather suggestive. By far the most attractive woman I have seen here is our hostess.[1]

Our 'visit' seems endless. We occupy two rooms, and all dine with her, while I for three weeks have had all meals here in my room, and even now we are made to feel our visit is a pleasure, and not an act of charity.

---

[1] Mrs Watson.

It's really rather amusing when there is peace. We three share a room and have our beds in a row. I quite look forward to the return of the others in the evening. Livesay is on the roundabout with Glubb to help her at first, till she was put to work in the store. Every case and bale had to be re-packed and new lists of contents made, for all lists were lost somehow in the retreat. A wearisome job though Little was in her element - a strange one.

Up to all meals but breakfast and ravenous. Dr Berry will not allow me to feed in restaurants yet, so I have for decency's sake to curb my appetite. A beautiful old general came to stay, unfortunately very deaf, and my French simply won't rise to deaf men. Glubb and I represented the lines at dinner and were amused to hear that the report of our discipline had reached him at Cernavoda. Where do they all get that impression from? - I have seen nothing to suggest it, unless it's our silence. We do not jabber when on a job, or when on the march. It was refreshing to sit in the delightful hall after dinner - Mrs Watson's brilliant scarlet silk coat was lovely by the uniform of the General. Glubb and I might almost have forgotten we were members of a unit, had it not been for our own hideous uniform with oiled shoes too much in evidence. We sat on the divan and drank Turkish coffee and smoked and tried to forget.

The General said that Bucharest had been bombarded again, by twelve planes. It was found that nine-tenths of the damage done was the falling shrapnel from the anti-aircraft guns, so now they are not used. Church bells clash and the police blow their whistles as a warning that all inhabitants must go to ground in the cellars and funk holes. The result is that hardly a life has been lost during the last bombardments.

Spent most of the day as usual sitting on the edge of my bed, writing or reading, too idle to go for a walk by myself. After tea I prevailed upon Livesay to come out. There was a grey mist over all. Earlier in the day it had rained, so Galatz was looking lovely by the light of its blue lamps. We walked along the quay, till stopped, but the streets were the most attractive, and we returned to wander there, where ever a blue light shone.

Mrs Watson in her car.

Tuesday 21st November

Rumours of every kind concerning the Transport are afoot. I went over to Braila to see Mrs Haverfield for myself. Fawcett and Turner[1] came along. We left by the 8 o clock boat which we just caught by pelting along the quay. The Danube looked more brown and muddy than ever, and it was bitterly cold. For the first part of our journey up there was a steepish cliff down to the water's edge on the Galatz side, and the usual fringe of willows on the other - the country lay as flat as Holland from the distance, to the foot of the blue mountains. They rise up out of this flat country in a long hard ridge, and end as sharply. One wonders what they are doing there, where one least expects them, but they are lovely. It took us just over one and a quarter hours to chunk up to the pier at Braila. The pontoon bridge was open so we had no delay. Being very clever Scottish women, we made straight for the café, but failed to get either tea, coffee, or chocolate - or cakes. At the next place we got cakes and nothing to drink. C'est la guerre.

The Greys were in good spirits and hard at work in their Romanian hospital. I did not get beyond the house they lived in, and lunched and had tea there with the brass hats. Mackenzie is on the touring car there, and during our drive round the town after lunch I was nearer smashing it up twice than I have ever been - Mackenzie took it very well. The streets were gay as usual with the blue uniforms of the C. soldiers. Their greatcoats and cloaks with fox fur collars make one's mouth water. Nevertheless I could not get away from the idea that it was like the Charing Cross road. It was rather. The object of my visit was to see Mrs Haverfield and get my orders about rejoining. It amused me to be hailed as the hope of the Transport, and I was surprised to feel so glad to see everyone again. There were three Buffs there. We drove to the station with Mackenzie to catch the 5 o clock train from Bucharest. It was packed. A kind but officious man cursed and fought on our behalf till we were forced into the passage of a 1st class carriage. Here we were nearly crushed to death by a Romanian officer who outdid even his countrymen in atrocity. He simply pushed his way along - we could have killed him, but no one else seemed to think it odd or annoying.

At Galatz we arrived at 6.30 and filled up the time before dining at the Opples by getting our hair cut. I hate it, it sets my teeth on edge - besides, I don't wish to have it like a convict's - each time I say shall be the last. I can't see that gollywogs are worse people than convicts.[2] The Opples is a very 2nd class restaurant, but our allowance of 2 roubles 50 a day from the Russian Government fits with the prices there. For that we had a ham omelette each, then a dish of chopped up meat and potatoes. We then tramped home, to bed, in the one little room where during this visit five of us (Fawcett, Turner, Suche, Livesay and I) have lived quite happily. How nice to have for dinner, say, oysters, hare soup, white bait, a whole woodcock, beef and Yorkshire pudding, macaroni cheese and peaches, then to sit by a fire

---

[1] Margaret Fawcett and Lois Turner were orderlies attached to Dr Chesney's hospital. Both were to ask for a transfer, Fawcett to Dr Inglis' hospital, and Turner to Transport, where she became the third member of "The Firm" of Ysabel Birkbeck and Hester Mackenzie-Edwards.

[2] Birkbeck had very curly dark hair.

(not stove), then to straggle up to a room, all alone, and then sleep until one woke of oneself, in a crepe-de-chine nightie.

Bell turned up again, much worse. I ran into her and had tea, and met her again at the Monopal for dinner. Suche came too. After dinner she went on and we returned.[1]

There is ceaseless traffic between Braila, Ismail and Galatz. Parties arrive by two or three and have to be fitted in, either to our house or the Bulgarian house we have appropriated, where Little and co live. Some of the visits are a pleasure to us, some - the reverse.

Sunday 26ᵗʰ November

Orders at last. They are in brief, Back to the Bulgars. News from the front is very bad. The enemy are across the Danube in the North, and advancing on Bucharest. All wounded from there are being evacuated here, over 40,000 are expected. All the churches and synagogues etc are being prepared to receive them. We leave now, to be attached to Russian cavalry near Constanta. We might have guessed it, for in Constanta is the headquarters of General Von Mackensen - I did hope we would be given to the Bulgars after Xmas, not before! Heaven knows what we can do on those roads though, and here we could work all winter in town. Well, well, this must be, but it's becoming a bore forming part of an experiment or an advertisement.

---

[1] This paragraph omitted in typescript.

Marsali Taylor, 2011:

It was our Shetland Film Festival that got my husband Philip involved. The theme for a local film maker was 'Heroes and Villains'

'Aunt Ysabel,' I suggested, fresh from my visit to the exhibition. 'The S.W.H women were heroines, if anyone was, and nobody's even heard of them any more.'

I'd also brought home a short ciné film taken by a visitor at Loch Hourn. We played it onto a sheet hooked over the curtain rail, and the past flickered in the darkness. A walk up by the waterfall, with Dad striding up, our Siamese cat at his heels, and Mum young and pretty in a print skirt. My sister followed her with a stick; I was the chubby toddler in red shorts stomping along behind. Then the scene changed and there, alive again, was the Aunt Ysabel I remembered, in *Mine*, tugging the engine, then turning to head off down the loch.

Philip combined that short clip with some other film, photos and diary extracts – her journey in the cattle truck "ward", which sent him back to the originals.

'It's not just the ending,' he said. 'There's quite a lot that's different.'

'Where he couldn't read it, and had to guess?'

Philip shook his head. 'There are some places where what your dad's got is clearly not what she's written, and he's added bits here and there.'

All that work to produce a transcript ... and it wasn't even accurate?

The easiest way to proceed, I thought (giving up being out of the question, now I'd got interested) was for me to read the transcript aloud while Philip checked the originals. I coaxed him into half an hour a day, after lunch, starting in the Christmas holidays.

It wasn't just a word here or there. We managed only two pages of typescript in the first session, and by the end of it they were covered with my pen annotations. I was worried about the originals being handled too, so method B was for Philip to follow my scanned page, while I simply underlined disputed readings. Then I re-typed the page into the computer, blowing up the j-peg to scrutinise these words. Sometimes it helped; sometimes it didn't.

When Philip became too busy, I worked alone, looking from typescript to j-peg, then typing up each page as I finished it. I tried also to reproduce her punctuation, going by capitals and sense to distinguish between dashes meaning commas, dashes or full-stops.

Instead of muttering about why Dad hadn't done it accurately first time round, I appreciated the hours of patient work it had taken to get a transcript at all. I'd never have started from scratch, as he did. The detail may be mine, but the whole is his.

6. Back to work again: 27th November – 21st December.

6. Back to work again: 27th November – 21st December.

Initially attached to the field hospitals at Ismail, the Transport were moved to the direct charge of Dr Inglis at Braila in mid-November after a disagreement between Mrs Haverfield and Dr Stanojevik, head of the Serbian field hospital. There were problems between Mrs Haverfield and many members of her transport. Dr Chesney's sharpness also caused difficulties, and several personnel were moved.

Fighting continued in the Dobruja. General Sakharov's forces re-took Hirsova, and, with the help of a division of the British Armoured Car Corps, pushed the front line back almost to Chernavoda, and the vital Carol Bridge. From 30 November to 21 December, the Transport were kept busy ferrying wounded from this new advance.

The Dobruja: Tulcea, Babadag, Cogealac.

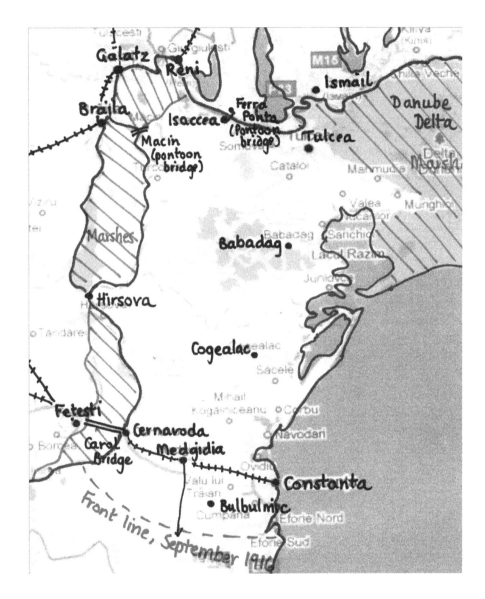

Distances: Galatz to Cernavoda: 90 miles, as the crow flies

Galatz to Ismail: 50 miles by water

Tulcea to Babadag: 35 miles

Babadag to Cogealac: 40 miles

Monday 27th November

Edwards[1] and I left for Ismail by the only boat, leaving at 7.30. We first missed our boat at Reni. A priest adopted us first. Then a Romanian naval officer of some importance took charge. He helped us with our luggage at Tulcea where we changed and put us on the Ismail boat which we just caught. We were rather disappointed at this, as he had asked us to lunch with him, if we had time - we were both ravenous, but no food was to he had. There were a lot of Serbs going down too, and their officers were picnicking at the end of the boat. When they began to clean up the remnants of their bread and cheese we could bear it no longer, and rushed up, and arrived for the remains. One talked German to me, and Edwards found one who talked English. Mine asked me what I thought of R. officers and I told him. He was fairly nice.

At Ismail they got us a cart, and we drove up in triumph on the pile of luggage, a pile so large that when we showed it to them, Edwards' friend said only 'Me God.' The river was lovely - a huge flock of geese were sitting along the bank at one spot.

Ismail is indeed "the abomination of desolation", street after street of houses, bordered by acacia trees, before low one-storied houses all made to the same pattern. Only the high road and main street are made roads, the rest just beaten tracks, knee-deep in dust and sand - and mud in winter. The mess room was very gay, when we arrived at tea time. A huge hired gramophone was trumpeting ragtime at a room full of Buffs eating a huge tea. All have lost the mark of the Exodus, and most have put on a stone in weight, I should think. After supper Hodges gave us our first lesson in ballet dancing. As we pounded through the figures of the "Buffer Ballet" we must have looked pretty funny. Most had field boots on and Suche came in in her pyjamas from her room, and joined in.

Tuesday 28th November

Pottered about the town in the morning with Reaney. The cathedral has rather wonderful great copper bells. After lunch Suche and I went a long walk across country. We walked straight away - along a footpath, through one small village after another, fiercely guarded by wild looking dogs. There are no roads at all except tracks, connecting them. The country was dead flat, and there were just enough straggling houses and scrawny trees on the landscape to make it hard to find the way back. The 'grammy' was in full blast when we got back - we never let it rest for one moment. After supper we cleared the room and Hodges gave us our next lesson in the Buffer Ballet, which she invented as we went along. It was too, too funny. Most of us had field boots and simply crashed about. Tunics soon came off, and

---

[1] Hester Mackenzie-Edwards, of the Transport.

then sleeves were rolled up. Suche came in, again in her pyjamas, and altogether we were a comic 'corps de ballet', if ever. We laughed so much we could not keep our balance.

Our house has been empty for months and has had no fires in it, so it's damp and cold to a degree. Even when tightly strapped into my valise[1] I could not sleep all night.

Caught a new flea - and a cold.

Ismail is really awfully interesting. Originally it was a Turkish town and their last stand in defending it was 1674. Russian gave the Dobruja to Romania after this war, and it's for that, that they are so annoyed with Romania for letting the Dobruja go again. I think fortifications remain and a Turkish colony is still to be found there. See Childe Harold bk V.

Wednesday 29th November

Up early, a bright sunny day for a change. The roads are still very chawed up, but have hard beaten tracks crossing at the corners so one can get about dryshod. The cars are all in a farmyard – no. 8 looked a new automobile, Jensen having cleaned her entirely inside and out. I had not seen her for eight weeks. The small engine was bright and free from rust and the body had been oiled and the Red Cross repainted. She started up the first turn. Really rather wonderful, this weather, considering they have slept out for months and months. Lots of the others have had to jack theirs up. I am accused of talking about her in my sleep. I certainly think a lot about her, at present. Mrs Haverfield returned during the day with the mail, and news of work. With so many untouched wounded, waiting is very annoying.

We are all to divide up - Hospital B with Dr Chesney to remain with the Serbs in their new camp, Hospital A to be attached to the Russians and work at Ismail, and the Transport to work for them also at Babadag - we are with Russian cavalry and work on high road, in connection with horse ambulances. If that is so, we ought to be able to work all winter - with luck.

I think I never enjoyed a mail more. Jim's amused me most of all my letters. No ballet, we all sat in corners in the mess room and wrote hard, while the 'Grammie' was at last allowed to rest.

Dr Inglis turned up late at night.

---

[1] She had a Wolseley valise, a trunk and sleeping-bag combined, bought at the Army and Navy stores.

Thursday 30th November

Dr Inglis harangued the Transport after breakfast. The first part was against the nasty habits of the T., the last a harangue. Although we were told our work had been very good, and the result, the Russians had asked for us for the winter. She pointed out that this was one up to us, and we must redouble our efforts, or that's what we felt she said. As a matter of fact she said, "Work on as you have worked, that will be enough." We were warned that the next winter would be harder than anything we had had before. It will certainly be colder.

After our harangue we all trooped to the yard and collected our luggage and drove down to the quay. I ran off to buy boxes for us to carry on the cars for dressings. The coffin shop seemed the best place. They offered me a wonderful silver coffin, and when I showed him I wanted something far smaller he showed me one for a baby. I got 5 boxes in the end. At 10 we drove down to the river in a string, and I ran over and killed a dog.

Our barge was just as all other barges. We had very few soldiers with us, and reed mats for tents. We were better off than usual, for we found our way down into the hold, where there was a stove. We all fugged there all the afternoon and evening. Suche got us supper of cooked cheese, potatoes and onions, and we just boiled there, till we had to go up to breathe, like whales. The smoke and general atmosphere were thick before we slept. Most of us slept down there. The little Russian sister we have with us to do the accounts for the Russian Red Cross slept with me, one on each side of the valise. She giggled a great deal when the others lay on the floor without undressing. The edge of all this will wear off no doubt, and she'll be crying about it soon.

Friday 1st December

We got off the barge at 11.20 over the usual horrible little planks. Faithfull's Burford refused as usual, and stood kicking up the planks that were laid down for her. Faithfull just backed her till they were rearranged and drove off without turning a hair. I hate it even with my little Ford. They leave such a yawning chasm between the planks.

After hanging about for two hours we got off for Tultcha. The kitchen car kept us amused. She refused as usual to budge, and then had to be towed. Once off, her driver could not communicate with her tug, and she buzzed three times round Tulcea to the delight of the town, and the disgust of the cook. We ran off to a café to get coffee but could get no cakes and daren't wait for coffee or tea. We each seized a lump of some sticky stuff and fled back to our cars before we were missed.

At 1.30 we streamed off, to Babadag. The road was fairly crowded but good. We had all put our chains on and they were loose and made a hideous noise. Some lorries passed us and cheered tremendously. I recognised them as some of the people that had camped near us at Cernavoda, before we started work at Medgidia. We have all been through it since, and we waved too.

We came to an arm of the Black Sea before we arrived. As Edwards says, 'We have most of us given up "admiring the scenery"', but it really was lovely. It looked like a lake among the mountains. As we arrived it was getting dusk. There were rich reddish reeds in the foreground among which a flock of sheep were feeding.

We all came in together and lined up in the street. Mrs Haverfield and the officers went on to headquarters and left us freezing outside. We stamped up and down for two <u>hours</u> and then got off at last. Our cars were lined up in a kind of barrack square, opposite army lorries. We left them there and trooped off to our quarters, through deep cold mud. Eleven of us went to the Hotel Carol, a picturesque inn. Here we had one room and a stove, and managed our usual fug in no time. We sat round the stove and smoked and sang, till our pitying host brought in a musical instrument, half squiffer and half piano. Hedges solemnly played hymns and musical comedy songs while the host pumped perspiringly. He reeked so terribly of garlic we longed to get him out. Hedges played the R. National Anthem and then Amen again and again. Then goodnight in five languages, to all of which attacks he merely bowed and smiled. At last we succeeded in 'bowing' him out. Two warm nights make a lot of difference, and we all felt the better for it. Amen.

A soldier was told off to wait on us and proved a very good friend. He brought us an excellent supper rather late, stew, brown bread and tea.

Birkbeck, Onslow, Hedges, Holme, the Sentry.

Saturday 2nd December

Slept beautifully in the warmth. At about 8 breakfast appeared - tea and black bread. After breakfast we went for orders and found we were to tinker at the cars, and move our rooms. My treasure started first pull, after I had prepared her. The usual R. army looked on with interest while we removed our chains, and so forth. Every car has to buzz every day whether going out or not. The kitchen did her usual turn. This time the army shoved, behind.

All the civil inhabitants have cleared out by now, but the place is full - Babadag is the R. army headquarters. We lunched at mess, and the usual sing-song followed, then we moved houses. Edwards, Reay and I in one room with two more to follow. We settled in very happily - a good stove in the next room warmed us by a hole in the wall.

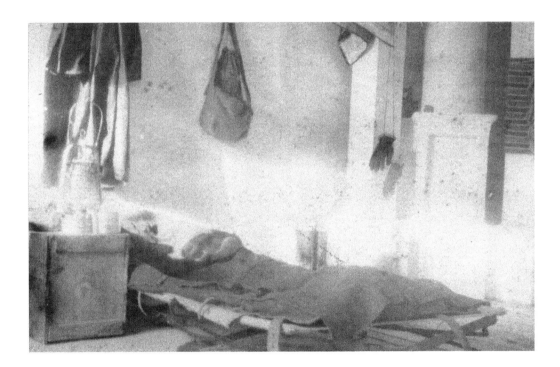

Sunday 3rd December

Spent the day pottering around the cars again. Bitterly cold.

All cars out at 2. We streamed up to the hospital, and cleared forty-five. Marx[1] had arrived from England the night before, full of ideas and wrote many lists of the order in which we would travel. I was to be last - however with Mrs Haverfield on board, had to get off first. We waited over an hour for the other cars to fill up, and one of my passengers complained of the cold every four minutes till we started. I had three and Little Sister on the step. Mrs Haverfield in my car led the convoy with two wounded officers behind. They were fearfully amused and kept grinning back. I, knowing too well the reflecting glass windscreen of the staff car, sat with a frozen face, with eyes for no one.

The road to Tulcea is one of the few "stone roads" of Romania. It happened to be a good one - usually they are distinguished from the other roads - mud tracks - by a few boulders chucked down anyhow with rifts and gaps between to wrench tyres off. Onslow stopped for me to catch her up and transfer Little Sister to her car, and I did myself down for ever by biffing her wing - just touched it, but it all counts. At 8 we got back - coldish - sixty miles.

Soldiers queuing at the cook shed, Babadag

---

[1] Margaret Marx, chauffeur. As an older woman, she attempted to be in charge of the Transport girls.

Monday 4th December

Filled up our cars then Edwards and I loafed. We are orderlies, which means we trample on each other's feet round the soup boiler and try to insinuate our flattened forms between the wall and the backs of the Transport with handleless cups of boiling tea. After lunch we went for a walk up in the hills. It's rather like Dumfries. Got back fifteen minutes before tea was set out and found Marx frothing at the mouth, as a general was coming. You get them here seven for 6d, so we could not enter into the spirit of the thing. Tea was ready on the nail. He and his two satellites were awfully nice old things. Edwards and I did not get a look in, as we sat on the boxes for orderlies in a corner.

As tea was finishing an order came for three cars for Tulcea. I, Donisthorpe and Carlyon went. My cases were hard hit, and I had to crawl. One was brought out on a stretcher with nothing but a bandage on in this bitter weather. After leaving them at the hospital, Donisthorpe gave a supper party at the café - we did not find much to eat except some delicious triangular treacle puffs and after a bit of wrangling tea was produced. Carlyon with Rolls raced Royce and I home. She got away first and I could not pass her. The moon was high, and as usual by moonlight the cars simply fled along. We got in at 11.30 - Donisthorpe forty-five minutes later – on a Stepney. It's a long thirty-five miles. To bed at midnight.

Tuesday 5th December

Nothing but car cleaning in the morning - ordered out at 2 to Tulcea again. It's one of the most lovely roads I have ever seen, but from a shover's point of view it was appalling - stones, flints, boulders, all have been shovelled down, in piles and heaps, or in beds a foot thick. It was a miracle we had a tyre left between us. I was hysterical for the first ten miles, then left it to providence. I had to wait till 6 to take back the doctor and sister. We all did in the end, as we had tea in the wineshop. My lights went out but I did not care. A staff car with a cinema lightwas in front, and I just followed it home.

We passed endless troops coming up. Infantry with their convoy of carts, their kitchens, their Red Cross. They walked anyhow, like a flock of sheep and with about as much interest in their faces. The Russian peasant does not care much for saving Romania though I doubt if all of them ever realized what they <u>were</u> doing and saving. Back at 8.

M. S. R. Regina Maria

Julietta Fotografa
Curtea Regala

The Queen without a Country.

Wednesday 6th December

Up at 6.30, to "lay the table" for early breakfast. We were wired for to go to Sariout about thirty miles off, to fetch thirty sick. No. 8 was rather tedious. We were all a bit bored with our autos and each other. Pumping water and carrying it in a canvas bucket, which slops the water inside one's boots at 8 a.m. with the temperature at freezing <u>does</u> rather darken one's outlook. We went off in the usual kind of way, showering sarcasms on each other as we filed out of the yard - the staff car leading, and Donisthorpe with her weak steering brought up the rear. We went South, round behind the mountains that are the background to the inlets of the Black Sea, as we see it from the Tulcea road. Again we came on the troops moving up. They mobbed our cars and we took on all we could. The lorries were covered with them. It was so horrid only taking so few. Again the road was lovely - and better, the horizon all round was wave after wave of blue hills. We crossed the range behind the inlet, through a wood - then on past endless little hill tops. These were all entrenched. We ran to look at some of the trenches - they were very shallow and the dugouts about the size of a fox's earth. They had been used.

Sariout when we arrived there at nine had a decidedly Medgidian feel about it - one felt nearer the front. Perhaps it was the ruins and skeletons of dead horses lying about.

The entire staff at Sariout met us as we arrived and took us into their mess. Here after one hour they gave us a delicious meal, all fifteen of us. Talked to the S. as hard as we could for two hours. It was a very funny party. At 11.30 we left to take the wounded. Mine were only "sick" however. I had a puncture and wallowed home in disgust on a stepney. Changed the tube which I put back with the help of a sentry, and got up to lunch at 3.

Suche returned from Braila Hospital with George[1] and the news that Mackenzie had sloped. Now, Mackenzie, Hanmer, Clibborn, Jensen, Monfries, Bell, Ellis and Glubb have left us.[2] Knocked up.

General _____ and his staff left for Bucharest, to save it. They had been good to us, and we are sorry - Edwards and I particularly, as Cossey goes too - a magnificent cossack without much to do, except strut up and down outside our house, with the <u>air of a cock who thinks the sun</u> has risen to hear him crow. Never was anyone so

---

[1] Their Romanian mechanic.

[2] Clibborn and Monfries had already left on 2 November, Mackenzie, Hamner (Suche's assistant cook) and Jensen went now, and Ellis and Glubb, along with Livesay, were not to go until 20 Jan 1917. Bell was still to be in Odessa on 9th February, with her sister and nurse.

anxious to "ger off". He is utterly efficient - then he clicks his heels and salutes till the polish ought to be worn off them. Such are the staying powers of Russia. We get more amusement out of him this way than by making a friend of him - besides, who could be pleased with a cossack who wore pince-nez.

Friday 8ᵗʰ December

No work all day so Edwards and I did our washing. George went out and looted a piano which we stuffed into the mess room. Two of the officers came in to lunch and one wanted a lift to Tulcea. He was rather a sportsman and was quite pleased to go in the Burford with Faithfull, four bidons (petrol containers), George, Mrs Haverfield and MacGuire. They were all packed in with straw to keep them from rattling too much, and set off. We all saw them off - rather a sight in the Burford always. Just as she was well under way, Onslow appeared holding up her famous fur coat, like a dressing gown, meaning to have booked a place in the car before. We all yelled and whistled, and the fleetest set off in pursuit. Onslow, hampered by her coat, pursued. George was the first to realize we were not being funny, and somehow communicated with Faithfull, who, being stone-deaf, is always hard to communicate with.

The other officer spent the day with us till 6. French and German got at him, and we all tackled him in turns, as no cars were out all day except the Burford, off into Tulcea. No ambuli are to go on the road till the stones have settled down a bit. They were not in to dinner and I as mess orderly had to wait up - at 12 midnight they arrived. Faithfull ditched her lorry with four bidons of petrol inside. A car came along on the wrong side, and instead of holding the road as the heavier car should, she fled into the ditch. Her cargo was deposited, and they got the lorry onto her feet again.hy

Bucharest has fallen, we fear - so soon.

Saturday 9th December

We prepared for the party.[3] Edwards and I felt awfully smart in the shirts we had washed the day before. We each cleaned our thinnest shoes and set out in our cars for Cogealac at 2.30. All ambuli went, and the Seldon. We were to bring back wounded next day. We picked up some soldiers going up - ten of them - I insisted on taking them. The road has become a quagmire, after just enough rain to make the mud the toughest most holding consistency. It was an awful drive. Like a snipe Royce zig-zagged along, snorting and grunting in an unusual and alarming way. Finally she gave up altogether and I discovered the exhaust had come away at the top end. Teddy[4] helped and we set off again, with no other cars in sight. Later we waited ages and four more steamed up. The roads were really atrocious. After Sariout we kept along the top of the hills, all were honeycombed with trenches. Finally we stopped in the road in the dark, till some soldiers came and we could ask the way. We had overshot the cross-road and when the others all started up and departed, Royce refused. The usual army crowded round and we explored her with a guttering candle. Finally she thought better of it, having I suppose cooled down a bit, and I set off to look for Cogealac and the others. It's beastly getting left in the dark. I found a friendly soldier in a village and he directed me, after much wondering and indignation. I found the others all lined up outside our temporary quarters and we hurried to dress for the ball at about 7. Having pocketed our shoving shoes and powdered our faces, we splashed off through the mud to headquarters. Here we arrived fearfully conscious of our comic appearance, and I came in feeling just as one does at one's first dance. In the hall was a band and as we changed, kicking off our gummies in a corner, we felt really on the razzle dazzle again.

In the ballroom, which was beautifully decorated with flags, were a crowd of officers in a bewildering number of different uniforms, standing round the walls in rows.[5] The old General was rather a darling. Cergazeff was very nice to us and held our hands rather tight for the first half hour. Can't pretend I suffered from shyness - it was too ridiculous for that, the only thing was to run in bald-headed. German stood me in good stead and we soon trooped in to dinner where I sat between a gentleman with a shaven head like a boiled egg, and Edwards's little Naval Officer. Endless hors d'oeuvres - then fish - chicken and some jelly stuff - the food was excellent. It was amusing to look around and see the Buffs all simply gassing away

[3] This was a party for St George's Day given by the General "commanding in that area". It was held 40 miles away - almost at the front line.

[4] Edwards

[5] The typescript has an asterisk here, and below is scribbled 'Shot as spy three weeks later.'

in foreign tongues. Cigarettes began at the beginning and one was allowed to smoke all the time. Cognac was poured into our glasses with great persistence. For vis-à-vis I had a Caucasian who chanced to have taken me out riding at Bulbulmic, and I remembered him well. His store of English conversation began and ended with 'Kiss me quick' and my Russian was even more limited to 'harasto' and 'niewazno' ('All right' and 'It's of no consequence') which I answered in turn. Nevertheless we rode for two hours together and never stopped talking for a moment. He sat and glared at me all the dinner, and insisted on drinking my health every five minutes. Meanwhile Edwards was making great headway with her Naval Officer, whose navy lived on the Black Sea. Altogether it was most amusing. In the middle of the meal the general made a speech, and they all cheered tremendously and drank to the English. The band struck up our National Anthem. Somehow it was rather sad - impressive - and one felt very small. Russian sisters came in after dinner and then the dance began. One's partners came up to one, clicked their heels, whirled one round in the wildest of dances, and then dropped one like a hot brick, and wandered off. The Polonaise and Mazurka were really an effort, but we were undefeated, and capered through everything. As time went by they all got pretty drunk in a harmless way. It struck me as odd that they were not removed, but none of their friends seemed to mind. I went expeditions to the dining room for tea. Then Cossacks danced into the room, in their picturesque dress. Long coats, tiny waists and shaggy black hats made them fierce and wild looking. Their dances were the wildest dances imaginable. They stamped and leapt with amazing agility and lightness. Later they sang songs that made one think. Without a sign of expression on their faces they stood in a circle, those unknown people, and sang in harsh rather thrilling voices, of love and war. When they paused, and I went to the door I heard guns and it - was it like the night before Waterloo?

We were all rather tired after a forty mile drive over atrocious roads and began to get rather sleepy. The last sene in the play was the photograph. Unfortunately by that time they were most of them so blind that they could not concentrate - a great deal of magnesium wire was fired, but I saw the cap of the camera was usually removed before, or after. One rather hoped the photographs would not come out for the sake of one general who fell fast asleep on the floor while the lengthy preparations were in progress.[6] He was carried out with as little concern as a dog would be by an orderly, and we all left at 2.30 and splashed home in torrents of rain, to our room where we slept on the floor on straw, and slept well.

---

[6] Hedges' diary has a general falling asleep with his head in Mrs Haverfield's lap.

Sunday 10ᵗʰ December

All woke rather late, and began chipping each other about last night's incidents. There was plenty of copy, certainly.

The cars started off at 10-ish with wounded from here for Sariout. All cars went. The rain had continued all night, and the roads were in the best state of mud, soft and squishy. We all arrived in goodish time at Sariout. Here we left our cars and crowded into the mess for the usual meal of tea, and sing-song to follow. They had heard of the dance the night before and were fearfully amused. At Sariout we separated, all going back to Babadag except Hedges, Edwards, Gartlan's and my car. Then I picked up other cases for Babadag and we returned empty to Cogealac.

The colonel who shares our house, invited us to supper with him. He then telephoned for the general, Radjen Arochidzee, Cerjieff and other connections. It was a gayish party. The old general raved to me about my dancing, to my huge delight, but I feel it was meant to be amusing. We all talked as hard as we could. These Russians are extremely easy to talk to. Radjen amused us hugely. He is ugly as sin and posed as the bold bad man, and recounted his rather lurid past and etc. Two duels - all for the love of a lady - had rather scarred his face. His rings were set with diamonds, also his watch and cigarette holder. Altogether he simply oozed money, and villainy – Edwards fell at once. To bed at 11.

Monday 11ᵗʰ December

Up early and to work on our rather discouraging automobiles. I got off first and drove on till I found I had shaken off the others and then pulled up to wait for them. There on the top of one of the hills, I could see away to blue horizons all round, broken by the ripple of hills. As I waited there, a long convoy of ammunition carts rumbled by, cart after cart, till I counted seventy, each with its pair of work ponies and barbarous looking driver, going slowly up, to the front.

Then came a dozen lancers galloping by and then some infantry going up. One sees regiment after regiment going up, but they never come back. Then as the carts disappeared over the next hills the sun went down and the hills changed to a vivid purple, before they were lost in darkness. All the while guns boomed, far away beyond the hills, with a slow persistency that made one cold - and then with almost a shudder, to look at the trenches all round.

The cars were caked in mud and none but mine would start. I had therefore the unenviable job of towing them out - the mud a foot deep. Hedges went off to

Babadag early, then after a morning's work, Gartlan and I to Sariout. The roads were far drier and therefore far easier to travel along. We each took three cases to Sariout. Royce was not liking the mud and had to be humoured. The usual people met us, and then we went in for tea, which we particularly wished for. My Royce refused to start when the time came, and we both ground ourselves out before a large audience. At last we got going as it grew dark. A thick fog rose and we made very bad time. After the railway crossing I brought things to a crisis by missing the turning and ditching my car in my sleep. She gave one choke and shut up, with water simply pouring from her inside. We were just wondering where the ever ready army was when it came up, this time represented by a derelict officer from Terra Verde. We made him push, and he got others to help, and we got her out – but without much water in her. He insisted on a lift, and I had to add his weight to my struggling car as Gartlan had some exhausted Tommies[7].

We crept on at first - Royce boiling - and I also with agitation, till the crossroads where we had to take to the fields. Here we stopped for water at a house, and as we might have guessed it nearly blew our eyebrows off when we put it into her, and I decided to give it up. G. took on my passengers and disappeared in the gloom. I sat and waited miserably for her return. A short examination in the dark reassured me that the jolt had wrenched the radiator forward and torn away the rubber water-joint. No real damage, I thought, but it does her in for the moment. After hours as it seemed G. returned and towed me into the village, to a yard where we left her.

We drove home to Cogealac, feeling anything but merry and bright, to find a supper party awaiting us in the colonel's room. Seldom have I been so muddy or so tired. We changed our boots and joined the others. The same party as last night to begin with - others kept drifting in during the evening. I gave a rather frivolous lesson in English to Cergazeff and a friend of his, and they taught me Russian. C was all out for games - he tried to make us play "Up Jenkins"[8] but we all struck - four months chauffeuring under these conditions has quite knocked that game on the head for us, for a year at least. We played a much worse game in the end. A game called 'Post' which really meant that people wrote atrocious notes to each other, in which they wrote anything too near the line to be said! The kind of idiocies I got were "Je vous admire de tout mon coeur; vos yeux sont les yeux les plus beaux que j'en ai jamais vus" and "Miss - please kiss me quick" - that phrase that everyone the length and breadth of Russia has learnt in English. The gentleman from Tiflis was in his element, and fired off burning letters all round. How we all laughed. We were all dog tired, but had to keep it up till 12 again.

---

[7] Presumably Armoured Cars men.

[8] "Up Jenkins" was a team game which involved palming a coin – the usual forfeit for discovery or a wrong guess was a drink.

The military situation grows worse - guns could be heard occasionally during the night.

Vous avez un bon coeur et
beaucoup de raison, mais votre
coeur doit avoir aussi ses
raisons qui la raison ne
connait pas.

Vous êtes très jolie
miss.

The road from Babadag to Tulcea at its best.

Tuesday 12th December

Woke to a world of mud, mud that is hard to describe, mud that works its way into one's boots, one's pockets and one's hair, mud through which one had to struggle a foot deep at every step. Donny, G. and I drove the touring car down to Royce and got to work on her in pouring rain. The yard in which she stood was two feet deep in places. It took a long time to get her fixed up temporarily, to get her home, and we got indescribably wet and muddy in the process. She started up first time in spite of water oozing out, and was winning back my affections when she punctured, about half a mile out. She was leaking too fast for me to stop and so I finishedon the rim and finally yarded her successfully. A hideous day. The puncture took hours to do. The mud was so soft and the yard so uneven I could not jack her up properly - and everything happened that could in the mud and rain. Edwards was a brick. The cover had to come off the stepney and the old one had to take its place. The pump burst, and at night when Hodges returned from Babadag with another tyre down we three agreed we were all for home, when our time was up. We have no doors to our house, our nasty damp house, with floors below the level of the ground and water trickling under the doors all round. It was dark and cheerless to a degree - moreover the food arangements have still to be made, and we get a meal at odd times - this day at 3. We tramped in and out till the floor was deep in mud and the straw on which we were to sleep spread about till our home looked more like a pigsty than a house. The doors have been taken for firewood – also the window frames.

The guns most perceptibly nearer. Talk is all of the retreat again - now. This time it may go ill with us for we have no petrol for the moment and my own is hung up till Donny gets back from Babadag wih my new water joint and a pipe screw, so we stop in our work and listen to the ever louder guns and wonder why we bother to work on our cars. The others had supper at the hospital. I shirked and dried some of my clothes, and got to bed early. Slept in my clothes as usual. We'll have to retreat in a day or two if not sooner.

Douglas Gordon Baxter, 1991

The writing is large, scrawling, and done at speed with various pencils. Sometimes half way down a page, there are interruptions, and the pencil that began it gets lost, and another continues in a different side of writing. Hardly any of the more commonly-used words ever get their full complement of letters but finish off after one or two, and sweep into the next word, that probably accomodated itself to the same inspirational abbreviations. The small linking words shrink to squiggles, or dots and dashes forming a veritable shorthand. When faced at the beginning with one of those pages, splotched, yellowed and crumbling round the edges, decorated with large curvilinear scrawlings, now bold, dark, vigorous, now faint and getting fainter, there is a willingness to believe that far from being readable, it belongs to some early script, written in lines, more or less, perhaps boustrophedoneously, in character not yet understood, and it is into this with a caution hardly to be exaggerated that the perplexed translator wanders, back and forward in an attempt to conjure up the exact words, until a flash of inspiration leads the way into or out of, the sentence that it is, and no others. Perhaps it would have been better had the publisher simply reproduced the actual diaries in their awful authenticity and let the public enjoy the vicarious excitement of joining in the action as they unfolded it from one trauma to the next, while engaging in the scholarly pursuit of deciphering.

Marsali Taylor, January 2011:

Dad. Boustrophedoneously?

I'm not going to look it up.

I see what he means, though; it's like doing a crossword. You have some of the letters of some of the words, and then suddenly you see the key word, and the whole phrase falls into place, Aunt Ysabel's voice speaking clearly again, as if she was alive beside me, on the beach at Caolas Mor. I see her dark eyes dancing, and the young woman's voice of the diaries belies my memory of a halo of white curls.

Have a go at her writing for yourself. This page begins with the last paragraph on p 122, starting: The guns most perceptibly nearer.

... was ... perceptibly nearer,
... nearly all ... retreat again
... This time it may for all
... as ... for we have had
... petrol for the ...
...
... with ...
... a pipe ...
...
...
we ... to work ...
... had supper ...
... dressed ... my clothes
... to bed ... Sleep in my
clothes ... well have to retreat
in a ... if not worse.

Dec 13 — Got orders after breakfast
to evacuate — This is ... to ...
... the retreat — ... to
be abandoned — All ...
... ... filled ...
... M.D. ...
... with petrol & ...

7. <u>The</u> retreat: 13th December – 2nd January.

7. The retreat: 13th December – 2nd January.

Meanwhile, the Central forces had crossed the Danube and marched on Bucharest, which fell on 6th December. The Allies decided, on 14th December, to retreat from the Dobruja, keeping the Danube as their front line. Braila and Ismail were both threatened, and the Scottish Women prepared to retreat once more.

This retreat, however, was considerably eased by the British Armoured Cars Corps, a division consisting of 44 officers and 455 men under the command of Oliver Locker Lampson, MP. The BACC had originally been part of the Royal Naval Air Service, and most of its officers were RNR volunteers. Like the SWH ambulances, the Armoured Cars were mostly converted private cars. The Acting Commander was Reginald Gregory.

The retreat from Romania: Babadag, Tulcea, Isaccea, Bolhrad, Odessa.

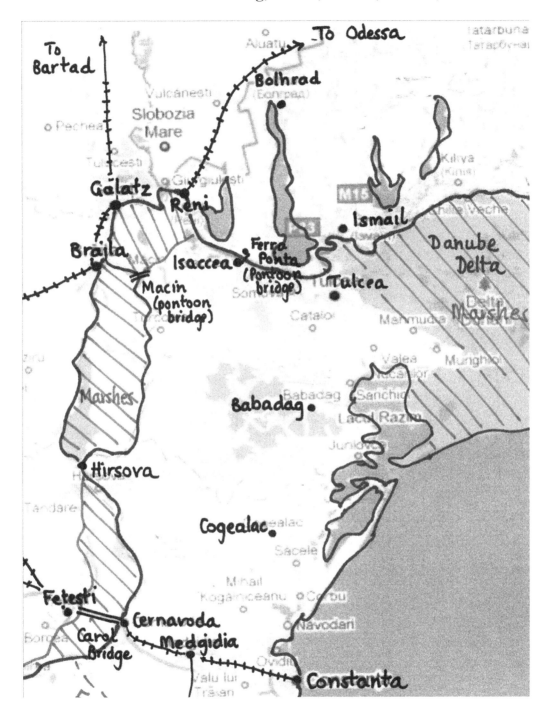

Wednesday 13th December

Got orders after breakfast to evacuate. This it seems is not a retreat but <u>the</u> retreat, Romania is to be abandoned. All turned rather wearily to our packing. Suche sat stuffily mending her boots. If D. does not return with petrol and my water joint we will all be in the soup, as we gave her our last. I supposed in the case of our not being able to get her out I shall be expected to do the Casabianca stunt in Royce. After lunch D. turned up. Where George is no one knows.

Away by 2 with all the wounded left in F. hospital, to Babadag. I started with a immense jug of water and three sitters. The jug ran out before I had got half a mile beyond Ferra Verde - however she ran on to a deserted house quite well, and there I let my can down the well on the end of some telegraph wire I found. The well was almost empty and the performance had to be repeated several times. The army turned up and finished it for me. The mud stopped the leak and the joint swelled. So after the first we got along well and I managed to get her in without a boil.

We stopped at Babadag to have some hot tea and get a little warmer before driving our wounded to Tulcea. My car was not fit enough, so I went with Hedges as her second driver. Two of the B. cars came on too. A thick fog stopped us all the way. It was bitterly cold, even the straw in my boots was useless, except when driving. There was some difficulty about taking our men when we did get to Tulcea and we hung about for half an hour. They were just beginning to evacuate their wounded, and would give no suggestions as to where we could put all the incoming wounded. We all had coffee before returning and would all have preferred something rather more bracing. It's no joke driving wounded with practically no lights along those roads, packed with the retreating army, through a fog. We got back to Babadag at midnight. Robinson's cart with the baggage had broken down, so we had no blankets or bed bundles, and our coats were wet.

Thursday 14th December

Lay on a stretcher till 5.30, when Onslow came and called us. All night carts rattled by in an ordinary methodical retreat. We packed the cars and lorries, and then things began to happen. The change speed lever snapped clean off on the Burford – and so on . I got away first, and waited for the Seldon by the road. It was too

lovely. Bright blue sky, and mountains, partly hidden by heavy black clouds - it's a lovely country, the Dobruja.

Holme and I waited hours on the quay at Tulcea till the others began to turn up. Barges were being packed with soldiers and lorries, but all very quietly. The chances of our getting off seemed pretty thin. They offered to get us off without our cars, but Mrs Haverfield preferred to chance it. As usual the most filthy yard was allocated to us and here we lined up and awaited developments. Mrs Haverfield and Marx next arrived. We lit a fire on a manure heap and stood round having tea and stamped our frozen feet. Quel vie!

waiting for a barge –

A halt on the retreat from the Dobruja.

Sometime after dark they got a deserted club for us and we left the cars there. We squelched into what must have been rather a smart place once.[9] Luckily the last inhabitants had put a drugget down over the parquet floor. The roof (which for a wonder did not leak) was very ornamental and boasted a huge chandelier. We fed at a restaurant till bedtime, when we lay about on the floor and had many interruptions. The halt seemed rather too temporary to unpack bed rolls. I had dressed for retreat in the morning, which meant putting on double quantity of clothes, for we never know what's ahead, so I was pretty exhausted after loading up the lorries, etc. We were all pretty beat.

Friday 15th December.

Breakfast, then we all tried to get clean. It is not easy to describe the state our clothes were in – so caked in mud that they would almost stand alone. Then the cars. We each had a huge pile of mud around our cars that we had knocked off. I took mine to a yard with a hose. We swamped the yard before she was much better, and I got awfully bored with Royce, especially as she picked up a nail on the way back. The inhabitants had seen enough tyres mended to allow me to mend mine in the street without boring me. All day a procession of carts kept coming in. The people here – the officers, even – know nothing of the happenings further up at the front' they ask us again and again for news. In the whole of this town are only a few Roumanians – they all ask us what will happen to their country, as children might. What will? They all say, 'We know you, you are with the Army at the front. Why are you here? What is happening to our Army?' It is the utter hopelessness of the whole thing that makes all the waste of life so heartbreaking. So few care. Illyachenko says, 'We can afford the men, life is the cheapest thing in Russia', but they won't stand it for ever.

---

[9] The rest of this page is from the Imperial War Museum typescript only – the last page seems to have been lost from the diary.

The first diary ends here. This poem is copied on the end-paper.

There is a dream that comes to vex our sleep
In which we fret & strive
For the strange gifts that time can give
    The pang — the bliss —
        The blow — the kiss —
The warm bright hopes & the stark fears
While through our shut lids creep
    The slow salt tears
And this I think is what they call — to live.

    And then, as soon or late
We feel the hand of fate
    That shakes us from our dreams with a cry
        A sob — a sigh —
We wake, while on our cheeks still lie
    The tears half dry —
And this I think is what they call — to die.

Marsali Taylor, 2011:

I'd only got to typescript page 37 (of 105) when I was sent down to the Aberdeen Royal Infirmary. The psoriasis I'd inherited from Dad, that had invalided him out of the Army, had flared up so badly that I was put on a same-day flight and kept in for two weeks, slestered in coal tar paste under stockinette bandages. I took the transcript, Philip's laptop with the scanned images, and my copy of Dr Cahill's *Between the Lines,* and in the long, homesick hours between tar-paste applications I sat down to compare the two.

It was absorbing work. The sounds in the hospital corridor and from the building site next door faded away as I flicked back and forwards. The shuttling between Tulcea, Babadag and Cogealac made sense at last; they partied, retreated to the pontoon, crossed, then were sent back again to Cogealac for wounded before re-crossing to safety. The trip to Reni was because Dr Inglis' unit had stayed there, within sight of the guns. I drew maps and dated them with the comings and goings of the sections of the Unit.

The comparison of typescript to text was fascinating too. Sometimes just doubling a word in size made it clear. In places, one mis-read word had sent Dad into a totally different meaning. Some bits, however I pored over them, were just indecipherable, and Dad's guess was as good as anyone's.

'You're very busy,' the nurses said, as they rustled in and out. 'What are you doing?'

So I told them. None of them had heard of women ambulance drivers on the front lines, in World War I, not even in Belgium and France, let alone Russia. Even the name of Elsie Inglis, one of the first women doctors in Scotland, drew a blank, except from one who'd worked in Edinburgh and heard of the Elsie Inglis Maternity Hospital.

By the time I was discharged, Mum's typescript was covered with notes, and Aunt Ysabel's part of the campaign was clear in my head.

The second diary

Transport seek not yet repose –
Hear your cruel leaders say
See the Bulpans round us close
On Till day .

Boiling car & punctured tyre
You must mend them by the way .
Drive your Ford & keep it going –
Night & day –

———————— " ————————   TRANSPORT SONG.

Box book

Please return to -

Mrs Digby.
Highfield
Fakenham
Norfolk.

A diary of a Ford Car Stunt.

The last entry in the first diary described the party being lodged in 'what must have been rather a smart place once.' Hodges described their new quarters as a large public building, with a gigantic ballroom; they slept on its parquet floor. The Transport spent two or three nights in Tulcea, then were ordered to Isaccea, then to a hospital over the pontoon bridge. On 18th December George Martin of the Armoured Cars mentioned seeing the S.W.H. in Tulcea at the pontoon bridge. The Transport and some of the AC light lorries left to go by road. C J Smith, Chief Petty Officer of AC later wrote of "extricating a motor detachment of the SWH marooned far behind the fleeing populace and in peril of capture at any moment."

Saturday 16 December

Finished off Royce's toilet. She's rather smart now - then pottered about the town, [Tulcea] and loafed, with no prospects of work - till 6pm. Then we had orders. Four ambuli were to go up to Arequoi to join a hospital convoy from Babadag. Edwards, Gartlan, Hedges, Onslow and I went. Royce started fairly well. Then stuck on the hill - fourteen times she started up with a pause of about 30 minutes between each attempt. The poor old Serb [Theodore, one of their orderlies] was nearly sobbing before we really got off, once the army lorries came, and got her going, and shoved her till under way. She then missed on one cylinder for a mile and then fired on two. Lights refused to work, the road was packed. I hit a cart, without serious results. Neither of us had lights, and the moon was not helping. We jerked on, along the edge of the road, till I ditched her properly. Theodore did cry this time. We sat in the dark until another lorry came along and heaved me out. They are great people these shovers, and old friends now. I finally arrived at Arequoi ages after the others. They were all waiting on the road nevertheless. We found the hospital convoy we were looking for had either departed or had changed its plans. We were taken into the Russian canteen, and given the officer's mess room for the night. We lay on the floor like sardines, tight packed in. Towards morning as usual it got very cold.

At seven we had breakfast - our own food and tea, out of the gayest little bowls and saucers belonging to the canteen. I longed to loot them.

I got to work on my car after breakfast and toiled away at lots of little things that weren't right. Eventually she condescended to respond to my efforts. As usual we put the cars in the one cattle yard of the village, and had to stand a foot deep in manure while we worked. The rumours of last night were that the retreat was a false one and that all went well. Nevertheless herds of cattle were being driven back all night, and as the day passed the traffic on the road became more and more packed. Guns - drawn by oxen - countless carts carrying hay - and other stores crawled in an unbroken line as far as one could see, from the front to Tulcea.

We had to crawl in first practically all the way. At 12.30 we arrived at Tulcea just as the others were rushing off to a hurried lunch before evacuating the hospitals on to barges. I seized George to attend to Royce, and we came back as the others got to work so I missed the meal. All our cars went out to the palace hospital and also the Russian ambuli. We worked to and from the quay till we had cleared it. Then we went on to the next hospital. The Russians do not go there. The four of us worked hard clearing eighty typhus cases. Some of the Armoured car people helped on the quay with the unloading of the stretchers and carrying them on to the barge. Some of the "sitting cases" were very weak indeed and could hardly totter across the planking even with help.

One of the a.c. men asked me to supper with him in his car, but I refused hungrily. There would have been a strafe about it. The S.W. work you like ten men, then round on you and tell you you are a girl, and an early Victorian at that.

Then the rest gave up as there were only four more in another hospital. Hedges and I each had a guide - mine was unfortunately drunk and led me along the quay till he bogged me in a morass at the edge of the Danube. It was about 9, so I was pretty short with him, especially as he refused to push me out. I dragged him out of the car and trudged off to find some of the English armoured car people that arrived this morning. One came along, and we got her out, and he helped me shove the other man off. It is too nice to have them here, and hear English spokenat street corners. They look so clean and spruce, and we are fearfully interested in each other. They congregate round our cars to hear of our adventures, and tell of their own. I went on after the men with another guide - a weary drive - and got in to find restaurants shut, and our food run out. No luck.

At 10 some one came for our cars for a typhus hospital to be cleared. Out came all our baggage onto the pavement again, and off we went. Ran loads till 11 - when I returned I heard we were moving off at once, to Isaccea. It was not till 12 however that we got off. The armoured cars came too. Two derelicts of ours went by barge with the rest of theirs. My lights gave out, at the moment of starting so I had to do it in the dark again. A pitch dark night. The road - an absolute jigsaw puzzle zig-zagging up and down the mountain, with too black a precipice on one side for a while. The road was fairly clear to begin with. We passed several camps where soldiers were grouped, asleep or standing round the fires. With several stops, we arrived at Isaccea at 4 am. The last bit of the road was a block. With one of the Armoured car officers in our leading car, we slowly bored our way through to the bridge. Oxen, sheep, carts with foals lying across the road and camp fires in the middle of it, made the last mile very tricky, being without lights. Once at the pontoon bridge we drove straight across into Russia once again. The open space where the others were was one huge camp, dotted with fires. We drew up our cars in a line, near the armoured cars, and some went straight to sleep on the stretchers.

Plimsoll, Hedges and I made a lovely fire, of which we were glad. We bribed our onlokers to get wood for us and kept it going from 4.30 till 6.20 when it got light. We ate some bread and one of the Tommies pinched some bullybeef for us. Gradually the others were frozen out of their ambuli and joined us, till all the transport were round the fire and many Russians and Tommies too. Below us lay the Danube, purple and black, and the gently shifting light on the pontoon bridge across which refugees never ceased to pass. With the light, we were off at 6.30. The Armoured Cars came too, but passed us and went north to Bolhrad. The road was rather bad, no stone road – across the marsh there was a bridge, and then a track, rather cut up but dry. We stopped almost at once at a Red Cross hospital to look for friends and found at Monastir Ferra Ponta, both the Sariout lot and the Cogealacsa. They were all camped together, and we joined them.

Refugees crossing the Isaccea bridge.

Spent the day dozing in the back of my car, and getting her ready for the next journey. From the side window I could see away over the marshes, to the river and the mountains - from beyond the mountains came the boom of guns. Must be the battle of Babadag going on - Cogealac has fallen, also Sariout and Babelak. There are rumours about Galatz and Braila. At 4 the bells woke me. I can only describe their particular rich deep tone as "Russian". They are lovely great copper bells suspended on four sides of the bell tower, near which I left my car. I crawled out aching and stiff and went into church. It was packed with soldiers. I stood in a corner near a wall. They sang their unaccompanied chants soberly. I saw the white veil of a sister of mercy but her voice was not heard among the soldiers.

The Sariout tribe put up an absolute triumph of a tent, divided into two. One half was ours, with our own door. Wooden beds, straw mats, and a stove in the middle made it the most luxurious quarters we have had for months. The walls were double and it proved as warm as it looked.. The other half was divided into 4 rooms. In one of the rooms we all fed, and in two of the others the doctors slept, and in the other was a kitchen. Never was such a tent. We had supper with the Sariouts at about 9 and went to bed as soon as we had finished. At 12 a slight diversion was caused by a Russian messenger coming with a note from some chauffeur hung up for petrol. The note said it was a girl chauffeur, so we thought it must be Livesay, and we all hoped - our mail. L's orders were to bring along the car from Galatz where she had been left, as soon as possible. So the long-suffering George was kicked up and sent to the rescue - and was pretty disgusted to find a Russian lorry. However it all pays.

Tuesday 19th December

Very cold. The Sariouts moved on to Reni and left us their tent, thank God. We cleaned our cars. Rather amusing, as the mud is dry, and one knocks off huge chunks with a tyre lever.

Sitting in front of the tent : the only names given are Birkbeck, Murphy, Gartlan, Plimsoll, Carlyon, Faithfull.

Wednesday 20th December

Perpetual streams of army lorries pass here going back. Mrs Haverfield went off, also Donisthorpe, for mails and orders. Edwards and I went for a long walk out into the marshes. The numbers of geese honking around made me long for the boys. Flock after flock of duck also we put up in the swamp. After lunch we all made huge plans for the peaceful days that lie ahead. Towards teatime Edwards and I took the punt and set out on the marsh - not for long. George hailed us before we had got out of earshot with the news that Mrs Haverfield had returned and we were off back to the front.

At 5.30 we got off, with the hospital unit, taking their people, and they our luggage. I took two sisters. As usual it was dark before we got under way. The track beyond the bridge looked hopeless in the pitch darkness. We were held up about an hour by traffic getting onto the bridge. They were coming by a better road, and I for the first time mutinied. I simply said I <u>could</u> not lead across that swamp. The only hard part was full of huge holes, that I remembered had given us all the creeps in daylight. Faggots were laid down over some of the worst places. I had to go - and got them across all right. The cars were full now, and several stuck, Onslow among them. She injured her steering pretty badly, but the faithful George hammered it right with a stick.

We all waited ages on the other side of the pontoon bridge. The road was atrocious all the way. At Jeletsa we left the high road and our troubles began - also the ascent of the mountains. On one hill four of us stuck in the mud, at an angle of 45 degrees. Mine boiled to the extent of blowing off my eyebrows as I attempted to help her. It was a horrible drive. There was some difficulty in finding the place. The real trouble was that the position had changed, as the Bulgars had broken through at Celic de Re, our destination, as the Bulgars had broken through after our orders had been sent, and none of the staff could be found. We arrived at a little convent in the hills at 1 am. Just as we were leaving them we had orders to fill up, and turn the cars round facing the homeward way, not towards the Bulgars. The lorry had to be unpacked to get at the bidons, and the packing of it, with George at 2.30 am, was the last straw. We got some tea and bread and lay on the floor in a cottage, and slept like logs. Even the snores of George never kept me awake after five minutes.

The marshes at Ferra Ponta, looking south

Thursday 21st December

Up at 7. The Bulgars are admittedly where we supposed them last night, just the other side of the hill at the back of the village. The guns give out an almost unbroken rumble over the hills to the stcatto accompaniment of the machine guns, and the patter of rifles. Very cold. We drove forwards to the hospital. I, Carlyon and Gartlan had orders to take wounded into Isaccea. We lunched at the hospital first, and ate like wolves. Our ship's biscuits and brown sugar had run out. They gave us goose. It's by far the most common dish here, and one does not wonder, seeing the flocks of geese about. While we were at lunch Fazzy came with orders for us all to clear at once. He himself was to return with his hospital to Ferra Ponta, on the other side of the Isaccea pontoon bridge. We loaded, and were soon off, at 2, with the others all following, to get wounded. from Nicolactsa where they were pouring in. When we got a little way on the high road we found the usual pack of retreating infantry walking in masses, carts in a single line, plodding back, wounded walking along as best they could. The carts had picked up all they had room for, others hung on behind. We each packed in all we could. I took three extra, and kept changing the less serious cases for weaker men I passed later. All looked absolutely expressionless, and marched in silence, bone weary. The pack thickened till we could only edge through a little way at a time. In the outskirts of Isaccea the street was blocked for a great distance with wounded, outside a hospital waiting to get their wounds dressed. We left our sitting cases there, and took the others in to hospital after hospital, but all had either evacuated already, or were evacuating. The staff of the 3rd division were just leaving their headquarters. I saw one or two of my "partners" of the Cogeleac dance.

We heard it was out of the question to leave the wounded anywhere this side of the river. As we were all consulting, Mrs Haverfield turned up with the touring car with lots of news. The Burford had stuck miles back with our luggage on it. Some of the passengers had come in on foot. We went across the bridge to Ferra Ponta. By now it was dark, as dark as it always is when we cross that _____ marsh. My woundeds screamed the whole way. Royce stuck in the mud, and the other cars disappeared. On the front seat I had a bad head case, delirious some of the time. Soldiers came out of the dark and pushed. Royce refused to pull - one of the coils I thought was wrong, but I could not attend to it without moving my passenger, and I needed one hand free to steady him. His face was covered with heavy bandages, so he could see nothing, and it was difficult to get him out.

We crawled along. Soldiers pushed, and she went a bit then stuck and waited for them. The lights were too weak to be of the slightest use, and I was in a hole before I saw it. Utterly beat. There was a mile and a half of it that reduced one to absolute pulp. The last part I had to steady my man with one hand all the time, then he fell asleep, or fainted. Could not find the place where one crossed the ditch off the road to the monastry, and walked up to find someone. I had to take my man with me, as I could not leave him. We stumbled on through the jumble of carts and horses that always surround a Russian camp. He came along quite well, with help. A soldier helped him at the other side. We knocked at the monastry door for some time before at last help came. By then I had got to the stage of doubt whether it was still a hospital, or whether it too had been evacuated. The monks gave us tea and their meat, and their kindness was very practical and comforting.

I found H.[10] fast asleep on a table, having just got across the swamp with wounded. We all decided to go back by the high road, and let the tyres go hang. They did, two of them - but I would rather have had four down than return the way we had come. When we got back to the head of the Bridge, the others had all turned up with wounded. I had to take on Onslow's cases as her car was wrong. I put the car right, and did it all over again - after trying to make myself drunk with my brandy, but there was not enough. How they suffered.

---

[10] Hedges, Hodges or Holme

When we returned, we arranged our cars to form three sides of a square and I lit a fire. Russian lorry drivers, infantry and cavalry dribbled up. We lay on sheepskins round the fire - others sat behind, and the outer ring stood. The back row were always shifting, passers-by came and warmed themselves and passed on. It was interesting watching the faces in the firelight. It was bitterly cold, once beyond the reach of its warmth. We sang 'The Long Trail' and all the old songs that keep us going and then we started the Russians off. One would begin, and sing a little and then all would join in, and always in chorus. We sang too, the songs we have learned. They sang the song they never miss, 'The song of the Volga', of the man who loved the Volga so much he wished to give it his most precious treasure. He threw in his lady love as an offering. What a people.

Prisoners filing past the S.W.H. cars.

Friday 22nd December

The sun rose at about 6, and we were away soon after. Royce simply would not start. For the first time I had to get George to start her up. The cars are getting tired.

Across the marsh - again - and northwards to Bolhrad - thirty miles. The road was just a wide beaten track, in parts, otherwise and pretty impassible, strewed with sand a foot deep. Again, the stream of carts and soldiers. I picked up a wounded and took him along.

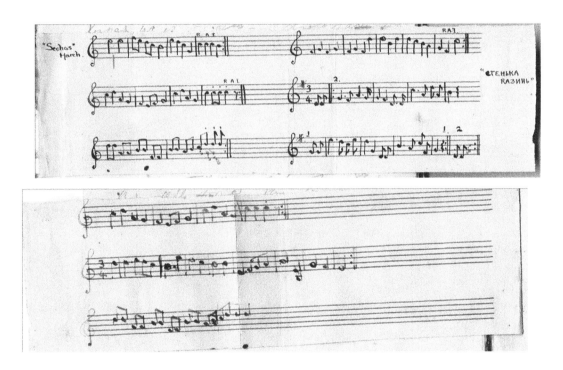

We jumped the bank and ditch and out of the road, which was too deep in places. From Isaccea we drove almost the whole way by the edge of a blue lake, which we all thought was the Danube, living up to its reputation at last. It was very blue. We stopped at the top of the cliff above it and had luncheon round a fire. It was very cold, although the sun was shining all day. It was really a lovely place, and lovely day. We were dressed oddly for a picnic - fur caps and things, but it was three days before Xmas! The country was much flatter - the bare low plain we passed through in the train, and around Ismail. The route was just one of those tracks we used to see, leading on forever without a break.

Road for Tara Pela — Bolhrad.

The last bit was terrible - sheer holding mud. We had slipped so often that as usual we arrived (at Bolhrad) in the pitch dark - and on such a road that matters. I placed my man at the hospital but he was turned out after half an hour, and I had to start up again and take him to another one. Royce refused, and stuck in the chewed mud of the village. It was defeating.   My guide carried the man the last part of the way and I returned to find they had all gone to a restaurant for food. We had soup and chicken - best food for ages - and then went to our billets and slept, on the floor. One can go on for ever after all.

Opposite: Faithfull and the Burford.

Saturday 23rd December

Spent a peaceful day eating sleeping and washing. We made three expeditions to cafés and then the bathhouse. It was like all the other Russian baths, half "Turkish". We all enjoyed it immensely, but felt very slack afterwards.

The armoured car people swarm here. Some left early for Isaccea, but returned. They took our piano away and locked it into their mess room. S. easily picked the back door.

Sunday 24th December

There was a very good Sunday market. There were street after street of stalls, grouped according to their wares. Fruit, vegetables, bread, boots, leather, sheepskins, coats and caps, pottery, scrap-iron, fowls, pigs, and stalls where all trash from boot polish to pencils and beads were jumbled together. Among the stalls the most picturesque of purchasers crowded - men in white sheepskins and women in gay coloured velvet coats lined with fur. We had great fun buying our Christmas presents. The whole morning we pottered there. I bought a long white sheepskin coat for thirty roubles, and a white fur cap. The coat we feel rather proud of as they asked fifty, and I am told that thirty is cheap. It is very beautiful, but smells too awful.

Edwards inspecting the pots.

George, Hedges and the loot.

Everyone lost their heads before supper, save Hedges, Gartlan, Onslow and I who sat stuffily round the fire. The armoured car people all came in after supper. We rolled up our beds, and really the parquet floor made quite a good floor to dance on. They came after supper, ten of them, and proved a very cheery crowd indeed. We sang, danced, played charades and various members of the Transport who could, did comic stunts. It was too funny to see Khaki dancing with Khaki. It all reminded one rather of a musical comedy chorus. It was everything to find other English people in exile. It's odd that we and they, the only English on this front, should be together. In charades we had of course "Burford", and did her being towed by 4 "oxen" in sheepskins. (Mrs Haverfield stayed behind at Isaccea and they told us they had seen her being towed!)

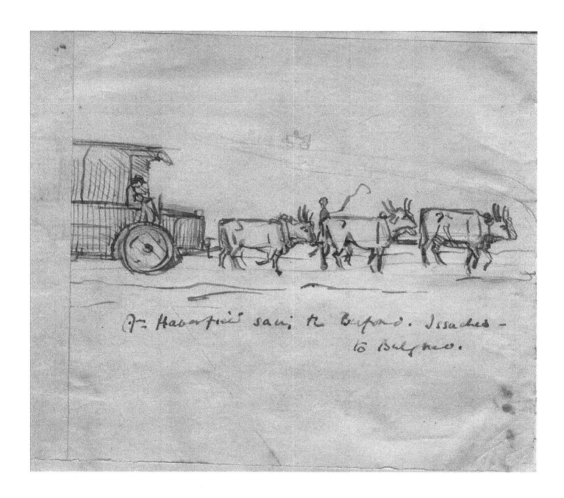

The Armoured Cars crew are perfectly mad. Hodges danced, which they hugely appreciated. They had several little songs of their own:

> We are but little sailors weak
> We earn but seven bob a week
> The more we work, the more we say
> It makes no difference to our pay.
> But Locker Lampson loves us
> But Locker Lampson loves us
> But Locker Lampson loves us
> and so he _____ well ought.

Their doctor was awfully shy and they never left him alone once. When he got up to say goodnight, they all yelled and cheered for the speech they pretended was coming. He sat down again at once, poor beast. At 12 we sang the Russian and English National anthems, and Auld Lang Syne.

Monday 25th December Xmas Day

Worked on the cars and got them ready for the next Exodus, till lunch. It was an Xmas dinner, goose and a turkey, bought in the market. It was rather a disturbed meal. Mrs Haverfield had not come in. She arrived after lunch, and arranged for all who are going, to go at once to Odessa. The rest of the day was spent in packing the others off, and rather sadly giving a hundred messages for England. At 6 they all left: 1 Donisthorpe 2 Hodges 3 Carlyon 4 Suche 5 Murphy 6 Gartlan 7 Reaney 8 Cunningham 9 MacDougall 10 MacGuire 11 Faithfull 12 Plimsoll.[11] The armoured cars sent a lorry down. Edwards and I went down and saw them to the station, but did not wait, knowing Russian trains. They got off at 2 am.

Tuesday 26th December

Bad news - Tulcea is flat. Isaccea and Reni, both no man's land. This place is evacuating already. Meanwhile the armoured cars have gone off again to Galatz, and a few embassy people remain here, waiting like us, for a train to get to Odessa.

---

[11] While waiting at Petrograd Donisthorpe was to meet an English woman doctor from the Zaleschiki hospital, one of the Millicent Fawcett units, also NUWSS funded. She, Hodges and 3 others enlisted immediately, and headed for the Galician front.

Mrs Haverfield gave a tea party at the café and we saw some of the armoured cars there. Most have gone to Galatz to scrap. One woman came and locked the piano up but we picked the lock, of the piano. Armoured car men came in after supper, five of them. I talked to a very nice little man straight from the Bush, Lefroy. All were Australians. We sang some of the time, but ended by just gassing till 11. A Danish doctor who speaks perfect English came in too, to supper, and stayed on.

We are a sadly depleted party - Hedges, Edwards and I in one room, the large room for a general sitting room, Mrs Haverfield, Onslow and sister in the other and Marx, Holme, Robinson and Walker in the other house. We three are very comfortable indeed, in our room. I looted a bed from the departeds. Ces sacrés Bulgars have mine.

Onslow, Mrs Haverfield and Little Sister at Bolhrad.

Wednesday 27th December

Pottered in the town with Hedges. We met a Romanian officer and asked where his army was. He told us with a shrug that "Unhappily no one knows, it is lost." The armoured car people told us that a Romanian naval officer had called at their headquarters, enquiring the whereabouts of his navy. They advised him to look for it on the lake.

Went to the top of the fire tower - an immense climb it seemed - after not having gone upstairs for 5 months. At the top a watchman stands all day and all night on the look-out. I fear the fire would be beyond the help of the very primitive apparatus we saw, long before he had clattered downstairs.

Bolhrad from the top of the fire tower.

After supper, Mr Lefroy and others came in - also the Danish doctor. We sang and talked - my corner roared about the Brass for two hours to my entire satisfaction.

Thursday 28ᵗʰ December

Mr Lefroy and Turner came to say goodbye - off to fight a fight at Galatz. Good luck to them.

Refugees pouring in.

Messrs Lefroy and Turner.

My corner, Bolhrad

Friday 29th December

Some excitement was caused at breakfast by the news that an attempt had been made to steal our cars during the night. Royce was found at the corner of the next street, the roundabout just outside the yard, and all the others shifted about. We were fearfully amused, as it was too obvious that the thieves had failed to start up any of the cars. The Selden accumulator was under the seat of one of them, though with the wire cut in half - perhaps he thought it was the way to attach it. Royce had certainly started up - the reason she had not got any further I discovered next day - I had left her tank empty, and they had put in some petrol and water too. The radiator of "Everybody's loved by Someone" was badly hit, two tubes broken through at the base, and some of the wiring removed from Rolls, but otherwise no harm done.

From Bolhrad to Odessa

Saturday 30th December

Left Bolhrad. After waiting a week for a train, we decided to take the cars to the station and pack into a horse truck ourselves. We drove down after lunch - or began to drive down - it was one of our best departures. Marx - still fresh for England - was driven distracted by us. The Sechass[12] habit having entered our bones it took us several hours to get the first car under way and the things packed. I spent the whole afternoon with George tootling away at the ambuli in the yard. We got Royce to go at last with a good deal of pock pocking in the carburettor. I then set out to escort Skally[13] to the station in Rolls. She had never driven a car alone before, and hung her up on a post in the town. It was awfully funny. When we got her off, she went one mile and stopped her engine and refused to drive her, saying she had "broken the engine". I got in Rolls, and she simply shot down the hill on Royce, as I had forgotten to tell her the brakes weren't working. At the bottom she got out and returned to Rolls - shot past the station where they were loading the cars - and I gave her up, and put my own in. The next lot met her bowling along towards Bolhrad again. The comedy was continued by Hedges who ran the roundabout on to the train, across two tracks and off the next, where it hung by its heels over a ledge. We then got the last in, when a telephone message told us the thieves had been caught. Marx had been agitating a good deal about it as her field boots had been pinched along with a camera and other trifles. One of the cars was taken off the train again and Holme rushed back to collect the spoils. Meanwhile we sat on our luggage on the platform or in the restaurant. They promised to make up a train later on. The train was made up at midnight with a few extra coaches. We made ourselves comfortable, with two layers of planks. It looked just like a wild west shack, with the boarded ceiling and stove in the middle. After the cattle truck of the retreat, it was a palace indeed.

We moved off towards morning, at a jolty lumbering pace of about 10 mph.

---

[12] It's clearly Sechass, both here and on the next page – a Russian word for being laid-back, perhaps, or – since it has a capital – a place where everyone was particularly laid-back.

[13] I can't read this name either in the original or in the typescript.

Monday New Year's Day 1917

What a strange place to find oneself in. It was bitterly cold. We crawled along with interminable stops at stations, or between them. We got out occasionally to stretch our rather cramped limbs, but all lurched stiffly back to our stove. We all felt we were off for the holidays and behaved rather tediously in consequence. Poor Marx was pretty sorely tried by us. Sechass having entered our bones, meals were a casual affair and we all leapt very brightly from our bunks in the morning at 7 am. Hour after hour we sat round a packing case, gambling at Slippery Sam - or singing the dirge of "We're all dressed up and nowhere to go."

You've heard no doubt
Of the Scotch turnout
Who came with their cars to the front,
They've been some time in this cheerful clime
Engaged on their Ford car stunt –
But now in Odessa they are taking a rest
And pleasure enough, I know,
But their sad complaint, that would vex a saint,
Is they've got no place to go.

For they're all dressed up, and have no place to go –
Life seems weary, dreary and woe,
Oh the life they've led, and the tears they've shed
When they've no place to go unless they go back to bed,
It's a sad, sad life and wherever they go
To London town at the end of this show
They will write to the "Times" and let them know,
They were all dressed up, but had no place to go.

[Carlyon's writing].

Edwards and I celebrated the Day by eating caviare brought in to us by Georgefrom the station restaurant at Bendery. We lunched sumptuously off cold stuffed goose. Since Marx's arrival we do ourselves pretty well. She is greedy enough to make a point of that - thank God.

Tuesday 2nd January

Arrived in the outskirts of Odessa in the morning. We were not drawn up to a platform. Mrs Haverfield went into Odessa for us, and returned with mails and candles. All sat on our bunks, simply revelling in our letters by the aid of guttering candles. I had twenty-four, and five parcels - a great excitement after none for four weeks. I had two lots of cigarettes and some very acceptable underclothes. I also had a *Punch* which Edwards and I chuckled over on our top bunk, till Marx finally blew out our candle.

Wednesday 3rd January

Sang our dirge all day long - and finally got the train alongside the platform at 4.20 in the dark. We were delayed by a troop train, which had to be unloaded first. The troops looked very Chinese and came from Siberia. Fine fellows.

Thanks to the thieves at Bolhrad we had very little petrol but decided we had better get off. Several cars coughed and gave up all along the waterfront and a car had to go along and fill them up with borrowed petrol.

Rolls had a nasty adventure. The car in front of her stuck in the gate turning into the garage so H. left her across the tram line and ran to shove. I sat in mine, and watched with breathless interest, a tram charge it at forty, and sweep it thirty yards along the line. It was a very spectacular smash. She was ticking over quite gaily after the crash, with her side smashed in and her four wheels sprung apart like a crayfish.

Quartered in the Greek school, a huge building of innumerable classrooms, most of which have been seized by various parties of refugees. We have one. Camp beds again, and a good night.

Douglas Gordon Baxter, 1991:

The Model T Ford was so ruggedly built that without altering the chassis or the engine it could become a lorry or truck, an ambulance - a bewildering variety of other ways were invented to accomodate its multi-purposeness. Designed to go anywhere under the severest conditions, it had phenomenal load-carrying capability and pulling power, it was also light and fast and made of the finest materials available. It was the single-minded creation of a man who wanted it to do nothing more than take his rural fellow-American wherever he wanted to go, carrying whatever he wanted to take, whether there were roads there or not, and to do it again and again without breaking down in any way that couldn't be fixed by the average man with wire, clothes pegs or twine, using only pliers, a screwdriver and adjustable spanner, and to take them in modest comfort, although it was often objected that the passengers themselves were the shock absorbers. From 1915 to as late as 1922 it was possible to drive all the way across the continent without coming across any made up road, and it was for the potholes, the rutted tracks and the mud that it was designed to be flexible, wobbly-wheeled and bendy in its body, instead of being rigid and unyielding. A lot of its success came from the great transverse springs front and rear, and the planetary transmission system, akin to an early form of automatic gear, involving continuously moving fabric bands; as a result the gears never got stripped, a failing in other cars of the time. It was lighter and more durable. It was worked by three foot-pedals – brake, forward, and reverse, and once the driver had aquired the skill this formidable trio offered, the car could be rocked to and fro, and ease itself out of holes, mud and piles of boulders in a way no other car could match. If things flexed, they didn't break up, and that too was part of the dream of a car for the people. It was the covered wagon all over again, brought up to date and mechanised, a rugged pioneer deliberately constructed to go to the same remote places and trackless wasteleands, through dustbowls and quagmires, over mountain passes, and it became part of the mythology of the American West every bit as much as the Conestoga Wagon. It was said of it that where Model T went, the roads followed, and in Russia with Aunt Ysabel at the wheel of Royce, it was no different. 'Roads?' she said at one point, 'There <u>were</u> none.' - a conclusion arrived at by driving up hill and down dale, cross country fashion, in preference to taking Royce over what passed for roads there, in the Dobruja. The Russian moujik didn't understand roads or how to make them, having no pressing need of wheels. In a land with such extremes of climate, few roads, and such horses everywhere, the wheel and the motorcar must have seemed to him a poor choice in winter, and worse in early spring during the great thaw that turned the frozen ground to slush then deepest mud. The sleigh and the horse-drawn litter were infinitely preferable to him for much of the time, to travel the shortest way possible between one remote village and the next. But for the boyar on his estate, a carriage must have projected an image of gentility and superiority, swishing along behind two shining horses over the brief sun-baked summer earth. Years afterwards, Aunt Ysabel never spoke of the roads without a shudder, but of the horses, she used to say, 'If you love horses then Russia is the place to be – or was then.'

Marsali Taylor, 2011:

We leave things too late. I have only a child's fragmented memories of Aunt Ysabel; Dad knew her well, through their shared love of painting and the outdoor life at Loch Hourn. Like her, he knew every otter's slide, every fox's den and badger's earth on his own patch; like her, he had been through war, picking up Norwegian refugees in Shetland in World War II. Now, I don't even know if he began transcribing the diaries while she was still alive, and if the changes from the scrawled word represent some better knowledge now lost.

My mother too, would have known a great deal, through Aunt Ysabel herself, through Dad talking, through her work in typing up his transcription. She once had the best memory of all of us, but now it's been stolen, piece after piece, by Alzheimer's, and all I can do is grasp fragments that surface involuntarily, as being closer to memory than I can achieve.

Royce, for example. The many women ambulance drivers of World War I used their own cars, and financed them too; the administrator of the SWH hospital near Paris had to fight to get salaries for her drivers so that they could afford to stay on when the war wasn't over by Christmas. The diaries only use the name Royce occasionally, generally referring to her as 'No. 8', but Dad's transcript calls Car no. 8 by the name of Royce throughout. Was Royce then, Aunt Ysabel's own car, which she took to the front with her? The photos show a gleaming row of identical cars, but the Model T was a common enough car for those drivers who brought their own each to have one. I had that impression, but then one day a piece of memory swam out of the depths of Mum's clouds: 'Didn't she buy Royce specially, and get it fitted out to be an ambulance?'

Dad's own introduction to the diaries says "She had also been put in charge of taking delivery of their transport at Brighton, and seeing that all of it arrived on the dockside."

If the car was new, then Aunt Ysabel named her straight away, perhaps in conjunction with Carlyon's Rolls, for No 8 is called Royce confidently at the start of the adventure, as they were driving the cars up to Liverpool. But perhaps she was already Aunt Ysabel's own, sent with the other cars to be transformed and re-painted with her Red Cross and SWH insignia, and called her nom de guerre, No 8, while in service.

The answer might be in the SWH archive in London or Edinburgh, but I have my own life to lead, my own books to write.

8. Odessa: 4th – 21st January

8. Odessa: 4th – 21st January

Dr Chesney's hopsital had remained with the 1st Serbian Division in Ismail until 17th December, and then retreated with them to Odessa. Their hospital was set up there from 28th December.

Dr Inglis, as always, was the last to retreat. She and her staff had remained at Braila until 6th December, when they fell back to Galatz. They retreated from Galatz to Reni on 4th January, and as there was a direct (though slow) train from Odessa to Reni, communications were easier.

Both hospitals were attached to the Russians, while the Serbian division rested.

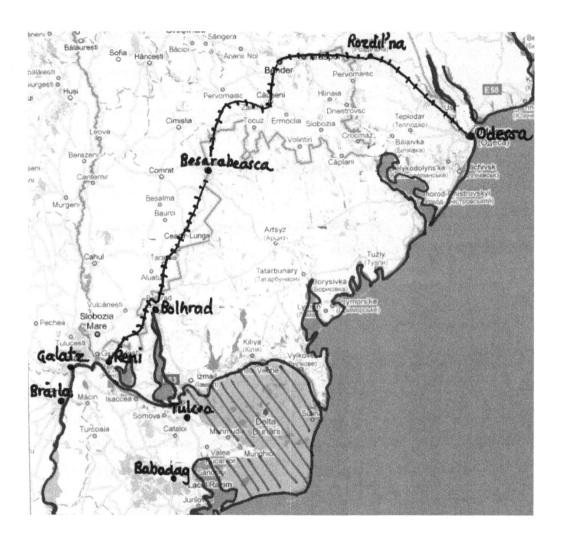

Wednesday 4th January

Pottered about Odessa, washed and curled, and simply loving the slackness. Edwards and I went to Franconi's, as we always said we would. There is no doubt about retreats making one very very greedy.

Pottered about. News very bad.

Shopped for our Christmas Tree - rather amusing. Little shrubberies at every street corner - baby Xmas trees. We all paid 10 roubles into the Funds to get one present each, which we were allowed to choose. I insisted on trailing everyone to the Thieves Market for mine, but it was raining and nothing was going on. The others all bought rather nice things. I will wait.

Choosing a Christmas tree: Walker, Holme, Birkbeck.

Sunday 7th January Russian Xmas

We all put on our "spares" and shoe-horned ourselves into our town boots and hats. We felt extremely smart, but probably did not impress the natives quite as much as we did each other. Several of us went to the English church, and roared Noel and suchlike Xmas hymns. The whole town was Xmassing so of course we felt far more as if we were really at it. Had a pretty festive lunch. After tea we had our Xmas tree, height 3 ft. All the same it was a very real one and looked extremely gay. The patients also had one up in the ward.

Monday 8th January

Our room seemed large after the cattle truck, but the walls have contracted since, as walls will. Round the edge of the room are our 9 camp beds[1], and in the middle our long table. There we eat, sleep and work. The chief difficulty is having nowhere to put one's things except in or on one's bed. It seems odd to start out in the morning in one's pyjamas and great coat, armed with canvas basin and washing things, to the "wash house". All through the huge echoing halls and passages, through silent swing doors that suggest museums and mummies.

Work began at the garage. Day and Percy, his 'boy', turned up long after us, and we were late enough.[2] All the cars are packed into a very small space, leaving just enough clear for one car to be taken down at a time. A very inadequate little stove pretends to warm the place. The doors have to be left open for light.

Holme, Walker, Edwards and I did not work. Cars had to be unpacked and it was an unpleasant enough job, sorting nondescript debris, the collections of weeks of wet weather. One handed out the object, passed it to the next, who passed it on, and so to the last who laid it down with a sigh. Truly we worked as British workmen should - and do - all the world over. Perhaps it was the greasy presence of Day that influenced us in this direction, as he yawned, and scratched his head over his bench in the corner.

Sechass has indeed entered into our bones. Punctually at 1, we knocked off for the full dinner hour. Dinner consisted of the orthodox chunks of bread and cheese and steaming tin mugs of tea - then followed of course a siesta - and work - gentle work, till we downed tools at 4.30 punctually.

---

[1] The remaining drivers were Birkbeck, Carlyon, Hedges, Edwards, Ellis, Glubb, Livesay, Onslow, Holme, Robinson and Walker. Mrs H and Marx would have had their own room, with, perhaps, Onslow and Holme.

[2] George Day and Percy Cowland were two mechanics sent out from England

(Above) Lunch hour, 12 - 3.

(Below) Lunch hour at the garage: Edwards, Livesay (standing), Birkbeck.

Tuesday 9th January

Back to work - valve grinding, scraping, painting - valves that would not be ground - scraping paint that refused to come off - and painting, with paint that would only go on in waves.

Bitterly cold. Had tea at Franconi's. It was well peppered with khaki - the Transport were in force and all the Armoured car people, mostly a new lot, but not so new as they used to be.

Birkbeck and Livesay, grinding valves.

Monday 15th January

Very few at the garage. I painted stepneys black from 9 to 4 pausing only for the orthodox dinner hour of the British workman and a short cat nap. Then threw stones at a yellow cat trespassing on a neighbouring room. Tea at Franconi's with Dr Scott,[1] Dr ___ and Edwards. Edwards and Mr Hunter[2] whooping it up somewhat. I of course told off by Marx to play gooseberry to her peach. However, it's not all boring - Hunter took a box at the Opera. The party consisted of Madame and Captain Cenderkoff, a very lovely little lady called "Nina", Edwards, Hunter and myself. *Dubrovsky* as an opera bored me, but the genius of Hunter in carrying on an advanced flirtation with both Nina and Edwards at the same time kept me interested. I of course was seated by Marx - I did my best to carry out instructions by holding one of Edwards' hands coming home, but could not of course prevent Hunter holding the other or prevent them losing our way (as I foretold).

Long day at the garage with absolutely nothing to do. Day is so unbelievably slow with the engine that we are all kicking our heels, having done our part days and days ago.

---

[1] There were two Dr Scotts, brothers, both attached to the Armoured Cars: G B Scott, Staff Surgeon, and Maitland Scott, Surgeon, who had worked with Dr Inglis in Braila and Galatz

[2] I presume this is <u>not</u> the Mr Hunter Birkbeck eventually married.

We are the little Transport bold
We always do what we are told
We never flout we never fret
We always earn what we can get.

We are the little Transport weak
We earn but nothing – naught a week
The more we work the less we do
The greater is the strait gone through.

Walker, Matron, Marx, Livesay, Hodges and Glubb.

Saturday 20ᵗʰ January

Woke to see snow on the roof opposite. Bitterly cold. Snow was not deep but very hard crusts. All the wheeled carts and carriages had disappeared and gay sledges took their places. Everywhere one heard the jingle of their bells.

Livesay, Ellis and Glubb were for home, so we all had a day off to see the last of them. Livesay and I spent the morning shopping. We drove about all five, in a sledge which was the smartest chaise I have ever driven in. Our cream velvet rug, lined and edged with fur, gave us we felt a fictious air of wealth. Heavy tassels hung from the corners. The horse too was dressed to match - a crimson net spread over him, and streaming behind him in the wind.

I got leave to be with Livesay, Edwards with Glubb. At Franconi's Livesay and I lunched with R, and at the other side of the room Edwards, Glubb and Hunter were together – I smiled some.

Went into the cathedral – it was packed, being a feast day. I bought a candle and made my way through the crowd to the altar to our Lady. Here I lit it and watched it burn – strong and straight the flame shot up in the still air – till a neighbouring candle, burning too, fell against it, and burned my taper through. A woman, kneeling, took my candle from its slot and put it away – I wanted to light it again, but left, a little unhappy.

Livesay, Glubb and Ellis left for England. Edwards and I saw them off. It's the sixth time we two have seen people off. Our room looked very bare and impersonal when we returned to it without them.

Sunday 21st January

Went to church. The snow is beaten hard as hard, and the sledges swing from side to side recklessly. The air is ajig with the tinkle of a hundred bells.

Edwards and I took Mrs Holman to lunch at Franconi's, then in a sledge to Arcadia. The road was hard beaten all the way, and we went along it at a good pace, till we got to the cliffs overlooking the Black Sea. Here we left our droshky and ran down the cliffs to the rocks. This year the sea is not frozen, but the rocks were covered with ice, and the most wonderful icicles of frozen spray. It was too cold to play about, and we returned by the same way.

Mrs Holman took us to dine with the Kesselins last night. "Anna" is living by herself for the moment in their great house. She works all day in a hospital, and lives the life of a girl of her class at home now. It was great fun and interesting to see that side of Russian life. Coming home Mrs Holman was jerked out of the sledge into a snow drift, which made us laugh all the way home.

Edwards.

Douglas Gordon Baxter, 1991:

Then there are the photographs that crowd numerous pages, taken with her folding Kodak, that bulge the diaries and so distress the bindings, yellowing and beginning to show the curious matt silvery-grey patches as the old chemicals leach out on the surface, and the sketches scribbled from behind the wheel of her Model T, of shells bursting on the track ahead, or the kitchen car in trouble, those happily speak for themselves vividly, without translation.

Marsali Taylor, 2011:

Sheltered between the pages, the colours of the paintings were fresh and bright, and the thicker paper un-crumbled – but those photographs! Faded, silvered, they worried me most of all. At least we had a typed transcript of the text; would my amateur scanning of these fragile images drain more of the sepia tints away, to make a real expert's task harder? Yet, turned from passport size to fill the computer screen, they brought the diaries alive: young Aunt Ysabel with her mop of black curls, a sun-bathing group on HMT *Huntspill*, breeches-clad girls working together to put up a tent, Jensen laughing as she washed her hair in a bucket. How young they all were, and what fun they were having, these girls brought up in sheltered Edwardian households, in a country where women were still fighting to be allowed to vote, suddenly let loose on this adventure. Oh, yes, the conditions were difficult, tough, terrifying, but for what was perhaps the first time in their lives they were freed to take responsibility, think for themselves where thinking was a matter of life or death; for the first time, they were adults in a man's world.

9. A trip to Reni, 22nd – 30th January.

9. A trip to Reni, 22nd – 30th January.

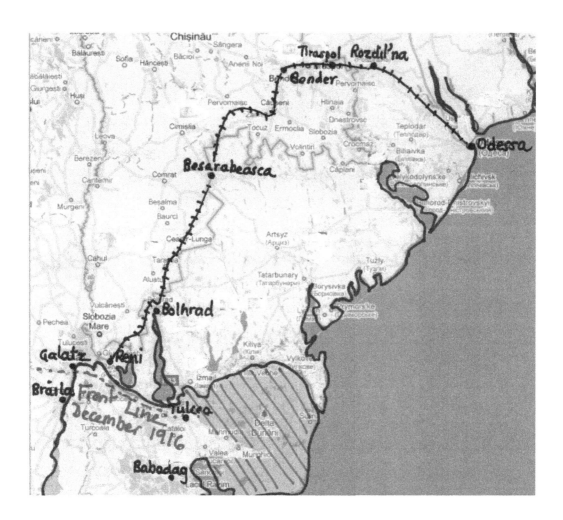

Monday 22nd January

Heard I had to take hospital stores to Reni, and spent the morning getting a pass from the Russian Red Cross. My French was utterly exhausted after three hours of grimly insisting that tomorrow would <u>not</u> do. Finally I found the greatIlneachenko[1] in one of the rooms I strayed into. He was just going off to lunch he said but I absolutely refused to let him feed till I had my pass. The pass came in two minutes and we left together. He was very amused at my insistence, and said he had waited four days for his. As he spoke English perfectly I was able to get at him, and tell him what I felt about it all. Like so many of his countrymen Illiachenko has spent a year or so in America. It must be rather a shock to such as he, for they are as far apart as the poles in temperament. It's the difference between the "Right now" of America and the "Sechass" of Russia.

At 6 Edwards and I set off with Theodore and one immense bale of pyjamas, my Wolsey valise, a canvas bucket of food and our two haversacks. We took the old man on to the goods station – Saslova – where we were to pick up the biggest piece, a very bolshoi[2] paquet – in the care of Marx. We found her in some agitation. Not only had the b.p. given her trouble, but she was distressed by the rumour that Reni was being bombarded and also that our departure was indefinitely postponed, as a train had gone a-missing on our line. We packed her off back to Odessa and settled down to a long wait in the station master's office for the said train. At 9 the inevitable kind official came and rushed us into a Russian sanitary train, which we only discovered later was not for Reni. After some difficulty we got into a carriage, the only one unlocked, and found four soldiers, NCOs and men – settled down for the night. They were of course fearfully kind to us. We explained in execrable Russian what we wanted, and they told us to change at Rozdil'na where we were due to arrive at 3am. After making the night hideous with his squiffer[3] for our entertainment for some hours, the man in the pink pyjamas had beds made up for us in his servants' side of the partition, and they tucked us up very comfortably till we arrived.

At 3 we were sent out into the snow, to another train, lugging our baggage with us, with the help of the soldiers. Some job that, as it meant crawling underneath two trains before we found the right one. We battered on the door of the train and yelled, for ages, before they reluctantly opened for us. The bolshoi paquet was discovered and to our huge delight, also old Theodore with it. He had quietly come with us, as a dog will follow when it's sent home. It was obviously impossible to cast him off at 3 am, so we shoved him and his paquet into the truck near ours. We made ourselves very comfortable in a well-warmed passenger carriage. Hot soup,

---

[1] Chief of the Russian Red Cross.

[2] 'bolshoi' is Russian for 'big'

[3] Concertina

cooked on the Primus, then to sleep, happy in the knowledge that we were in the right train and had the b.p. still with us.

Tuesday, 23rd January

Breakfast at 9. A great and satisfactory feeling of peace upon us, being far from the madding crowd. The canvas bucket does not hold a lot of food for three – we supplemented our store during the day with two immense loaves of bread, sponge cake and caviare – the last bought at Bender, where we spent the whole day, jolting backwards and forwards through the station. Snow fell at intervals, and except for our foraging expeditions we did not leave the grateful warmth of our cabin. The only other fellow traveller, a doctor it seemed, called on us twice with a kettle full of tea, and we held a bright conversation with him, each in our own tongues. The guard came and weakly expostulated against the Primus but we told him with smiles that we did not understand Russian.

Wednesday 24th January

Woke to find ourselves still at Bender. After breakfast one or two Russian sisters and two officers got into our carriage, but not at our end. They do not make much difference really but it was nice having the whole thing to ourselves. During the afternoon the soldier servant appeared with two strings of maize rolled in sugar. While we were eating them the two officers came and looked on, and then settled down for the rest of the afternoon. Really it was very funny. Neither could speak any language but their own, Caucasian and Russian. We had a phrase book, Russian / English, and contrived to carry on an amazingly progressive conversation. They played with everything they could see including Edwards' Kodak, and, of course, let it fall by mistake, to her utter disgust. However he scrabbled through the book till he found 'Excuse me", and I followed with "Let us shake hands and say no more about it". The sisters held coldly aloof.

The country was flat and wooded all day. The landscape looked like a pen and ink drawing. Black trees – white ground – reaching to a colourless sky.

Our visitors called again with more food and our friendship progressed in leaps and bounds – so much so that we were rather glad when the Russian sisters joined us after supper. The Russian – Basil Vasseli – played the mandolin and hummed love songs till the Russian sisters got up to go, and Edwards had the inspiration to say goodnight to the rest. We slept well.

Thursday 26th January

Roused by the Caucasian calling "Mees Ysabella" to find we were at Bessarabia and had to change. The line we were on was stopped – it was not easy to understand why. We all bundled out by the side of the line and waited for a cart to come along. Alexandre commandeered it for all the luggage, and we tramped along the line to the station. Alexandre made us all march and kept us very strictly in order, all the way. I have never laughed so much: we looked an odd enough party – Edwards and I in the khaki of Anglishki chauffeur, the Russian sisters in the white veil of their uniform – the Russian and Caucasian marching at the side of their little troop – all dragging our nondescript small luggage with us. Alexandre dragged me all over the place to watch them arrange for the next train. I really do not know what we should have done without these people. We left the sister at Bessarabia with great regret. She had been wounded in the head, and like us had short hair. Wonderful people are the Russian sisters!

At last we found a train and oddly enough an old friend, one of the officers on the staff of General Vaches of Cogealac memory. I had rather particularly liked him at the dance. Edwards – I – our two friends – and the two other inhabitants of the carriage got on well together. The mandolin man came to call several times and they all helped us through what would have been a terribly tedious day very creditably. The Caucasian is the most indefatiguable "player" I ever saw. He is just like Franz Hals' "Laughing Cavalier" to look at, tall and thin. He kept things going and ended the day by proposing to me, and giving me his badges. I have only six S.W.H. so would not part, lest I find six people more interesting. Conversation was easier as one of the officers we found in the train could speak French and translated it all for us.

We heard much of the war, and of interest. In the evening we heard that the train had changed its mind, and was not going beyond Ternoval. The fourth change – what a journey.

Our food supply was running very low, but the commander of the train sent a soldier out to forage for us, and he returned with four eggs, a loaf of bread and a cooked fowl. A very welcome change to a diet of bread and soup. We played a game of hiding a ring on a string – we six for hours – I never saw children enjoy a game more. We laughed till we had to stop. Ternoval never got any nearer – we were due to arrive in an hour when we said goodnight at 9, but it was 1 next morning before we arrived. We let ourselves – and our luggage – down onto the line into deep snow. It was snowing hard and bitterly cold. I did not suffer much though on the tramp to the station as the journey was under the magnificent Caucasian coat of Alexandre. They are huge black circular capes, of felt, nearly to the ground and large enough to shelter at least three people at once. We were the only arrivals, and found the restaurant full of travellers sleeping in every position of discomfort. There is no civil population it seems - as usual, everyone was either a soldier or a 'soeur'. Tea was most refreshing. Not so very long ago we spent hours here, when we left Bolgrad, on a journey through Russia. One seems to spend half one's life in Russia by the line, andthe other half in restaurants – waiting – waiting. We waited here for two hours and saw the last of one of our friends – Basil Vasseli. He saw us into the train and then left us to struggle with his own journey to Galatz, to the front.

The heat of our new train was terrific, and from floor to ceiling it was packed with snoring people. Alexandre turned one wretched man off his bunk, so that Edwards and I should be next each other.

At 10 we arrived at Reni and asked in vain for the English hospital. We left our luggage with Theodore and Alexandre's soldier servant and we three set off to look for the staff headquarters of Alexandre's regiment. It was a long tramp, down aroad packed with traffic. The civil population was evacuating en masse – a less depressing sight in snow than in rain. At Alexandre's headquarters we heard where our hospital was, and said goodbye to him with real regret. After struggling with one's own affairs for so long it is delightful to have people breaking their necks to carry one's haversacks etc.

Of course we were lucky, one always is if one is prepared to spread oneself, and how is one to get along on a stunt like this, where one leans utimately on the kindness of chance aquaintances, unless one does lay oneself out? The principle might be bad, but it's the only way that works, if one is shot off alone in a foreign land at war, with no rights behind one.

A drawing of Alexandre's insignia?

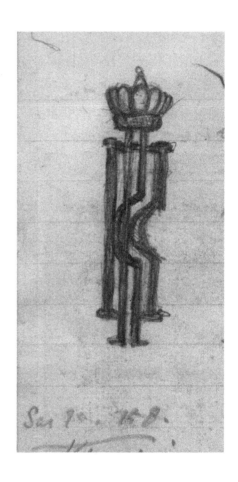

11th January 1916[1]: Alexandre's letter, written in Georgian in the diary:

Today, when I was going on the battle-front in Romania, have met two girls. After making acquaintance with them I found out that they were chauffeurs from England. We've travelled together from Bender to Odessa. We spoke a lot, socialized with each other and for the farewell I wrote this little memorable verse in this notebook:

"I dedicate my hand writing as a gift, may it stay with you to remember my name.

And if death will put me in the cold grave

Then your innocent tears would drop as dew on my hand writing."

Alexandre Khurtsidze[2]

---

[1] Alexandre is using the Julian calendar.

[2] I would like to thank Ms. Marine Tigishvili, the PA to the Consul of Georgia, London, for her translation of this note in the diary.

The hospital at Reni.

Hospital laundry, Reni.

At Reni we were given a rousing welcome at Dr Inglis's hospital, and a good meal, then rushed off to the baths. It's worth spending five nights in one's clothes, if only for the delight of a Russian bath after it.

At tea the Russians who run a sanitary train turned up and offered to take us on their train to Odessa. It was a little sudden but we knew it behoved us to go. We set out with them after tea – Edwards, Turner and I, with the hospital orderly staggering under our baggage and Theodore carrying our bucket of food.[1] At the station we waited some time, and picked up the sisters belonging to the train. They had been for a jaunt to Galatz with some officers – for three days. We learned soon that the train had been moved, and set out again to tramp another five versts along the line. The snow was very deep in places and fresh snow was falling all the time. I had perhaps the nastiest "turn" of my life, when I realized that one of the sisters was quite drunk! At 9 we reached the train at last, and very slow we were too. We three had a first-class compartment to ourselves. The whole train gave me far more the feeling of a pleasure yacht than anything else. The mess where we dined at 10, was like the best hotel – excellent food, beautifully arranged. This train, like most others of its kind, I think was owned by a Tzar family member – in this case Prince Constantin Constantinovitch. A representative of the family always travels on it. Everything is of the best, and arranged for the utmost comfort. We have fallen on our feet again, this time through the reflected glory of Holme and Hedges, who had travelled on it to Odessa some weeks before.

Saturday 27th January

Woke to find ourselves moved back into the station! Breakfast at 9.10! During the morning sixteen wounded came on (officers), and we got away soon after, to pick up the rest later on.

Lunch was a terrific effort, fearfully hot, and we cannot do the right thing. They use all the opposite tools to what one would expect - also they won't talk to us. Our best efforts in French are ignored. Whether we fall terribly flat after the others, or, as Edwards suggests, perhaps they are afraid that with a little encouragement we shall behave as they did, we don't know. At any rate, we fail to amuse or entertain, like the others. They told us great stories of snow fights and such like. We look at all these proper people and wonder who rolled who! It's all a great strain. We three simply sit in a row, and drip with agitation. It's not that their habits are prettier than ours, they aren't – it's that they are different. I would gladly spit and pick my teeth with the rest, if I thought it would make me feel more in it.

---

[1] Turner was now attached to the Transport – she had asked for a transfer. Holme and Hedges were sent back to Reni to replace her. Turner's terrier Sammy, now the Unit's 'Official Dog' was left behind with Clare Murphy's black kitten, Pushkin, as Turner was now under 'military discipline' (Mrs Haverfield and Marx?) and pets were not permitted. Sammy followed her to the station.

Meals are at odd times – lunch yesterday, we gave up all hope of at 2.30. We were all hungry after the lean days on the way up, so we locked the door of our cabin, and surreptitiously ate our cold fowl. No sooner had we eaten it, and dropped the bones out of the window, than lunch was announced. We struggled manfully with an enormous meal.

Sunday 28th January

Trailed into breakfast feeling faint and exhausted after a stifling night, and was utterly routed by the explosion of a rotten egg in my face. However being a true Scottish Woman I gulped down 2 raw eggs after it, before rushing away and being terribly sick.

After breakfast sister Natalie de Hincenlieff took us over the further end of the train to the hospital. Here were truck after truck. First we passed through the cabin of the forty hospital orderlies – "sanitars". They do all the unskilled labour of the hospitals. Then came the quarters for officers. On either side of the passage were two rows of stretchers one above the other. The stretchers were well sprung and looked comfortable, but all the patients were fully dressed in their dress uniforms – that seemed rather uncomfortable for a journey of three or four days in bed.

Next came the theatre and dressing room. Here all was spotless, and it had all the air of a stationary hospital. Glass cases of instruments – sterilizers and all the terribly familiar paraphernalia. All dressings are done here, the patients being carried in on their stretchers. They arrive here first too – through the big double door, and are washed in the bath room before being put on their stretchers in the ward.[1] After the theatre came the nurses' quarters. Terribly crowded according to our ideas. They were arranged in three storeys one above the other, as close as they could lie – side by side – their feet inwards and their heads to the outer wall of the train. It was not easy to get at any except the top row – which is no doubt why they all go to bed dressed. The train holds 500, and at a push 530. When we saw it, there were 450 and it seemed full indeed. The heat was stifling.

We picked up the wounded at Bender. Here we went over the "T__", an immense dressing station by the railway line. The neighbouring hospital examines them at this point, collecting till a train arrives before it. They were carried straight from the hospital to the train.[2] I looked with new interest at the sister when I realized she had been working here for over two years without a holiday.

The work comes all at once, and while she has any serious cases, Sister Natalie hardly sleeps at all, working and watching night and day, till the journey is safely over. Then on the return to the fronts, she sleeps, night and day.

---

[1] The second half of this sentence is interpolated into the typescript

[2] The preceding sentences were interpolated into the typescript.

They are such an extraordinary mixture these Russian sisters.

Taking on the wounded.

Spent the rest of the day shut in our cabin singing hymns A & M and our own parodies. We achieved another to-day, rather a triumph of idiocy, but amusing to us:

> All the armies love us
> All the armies love us
> All the armies love us
> We often wonder why.
>
> The Ruskies love us this we know
> For they often tell us so
> Where'er we work, where'er we go
> Transport – ochen harasko.[1]
>
> Ja vas labler
> Ja vas labler
> Ja vas labler
> Is the only phrase we know.[2]

Monday 29th January

Spent the day either jolting reluctantly along towards Odessa, or playing in the snow. It has hardly stopped snowing since it first began, about ten days ago. Now the snow is knee deep, and the peasants' carts are all on runners.

We arrived at Tiraspol at about 5, and leapt out to look for the Armoured Cars in vain, so returned as usual to our den, and plotted plots – more hair-brained than usual.

Tuesday 30th January

During the night we only travelled 5 versts. Men are clearing the line by hand before us, but even with a second engine, we hardly progress at all. Further north the snow is far deeper, but they are prepared for it there. Here however they have no snow plough.

"Father" – the stuffy old judge at the head of the show – is decidedly thawing - comes into our cabin and harangues us in very fprosy French by the hour. We all stop smoking and sit bolt upright, lips slightly parted in what we hope is a smile of interest. He began reading a Russian paper to us in French and we so over-did the

---

[1] To the tune 'Jesus loves us' – ochen harasko means very good. My thanks are due to Derick Herning for this translation, and the one on p 177.

[2] "ya vas lyublu" - "I love you".

part, that he read the whole thing, including births, deaths and marriages through to us. Only the timely appearance of one of the sisters saved us from "Situations vacant."

At 4.30 we arrived at Saslova and changed there into a passenger train, which brought us back to Odessa. Our trip to Reni and back took us 9 days and nights and we were thoroughly glad to get back again, to our mail. The snow in Odessa was very much deeper and we thought the cold, as we drove back from the station to the school. even more painful than anything we had felt before. The bitter wind cut like a knife. We hear the temperature is to drop to 37 degrees of frost – most unusual for Odessa.

Found a big mail, and among other bombs, the announcement of Judith's engagement to Jack Thornton. Marriage, Death and division make barren our lives.

10. Odessa: 31st January – 1st March.

10. Odessa: 31st January – 1st March.

Wednesday 31ˢᵗ January

Got a day off. We three[1] spent it very happily in shopping, and shop nosing. The shops of Odessa are terribly attractive. We lunched and tea'd at Franconi's, but saw no one of interest.

Thursday 1ˢᵗ February

Back to the garage. No 1 touring car is up, body and all. She looks very smart. The garage was almost impossibly cold – everything we touched stung our fingers till they were too numb to feel. Studdy[2] is to be taken down and high time too. A Russian sister we had first met at Medjidia, and found again yesterday, came to lunch. She was nine months with the Russian army as a soldier, till seriously wounded in the head. Now, she works with them as a "sister" which means whatever you choose to make it. Her short hair was curly, and her hands a revelation to us. Altogether she looked most attractive. We asked how she had joined. After making up her mind, she got hold of some soldier's clothes from some officer, dressed herself like one of themselves, with shaven head, and unknown to anyone, slipped into a troop train taking two regiments to the front. At the end of the journey the soldiers told their officer, and he applied to let her stay. Officially it is supposed necessary to get a permit from the Tzar. About 8000 Russian women are serving as men.

She told of a rather interesting captive. A small group of Austrians was taken prisoner – and one of these was found to be a woman also!

On the return from Medgidia one of the Buffs had met this girl with her friend – at Caroverrat, running a little dressing station by themselves. They worked there night and day, staying till the last, and so losing their all. Now she is attached to the First Serbian Divison. Russia holds many surprises.

Bitter, bitter cold. The Black Sea is freezing far out from the shore, and the wind that blows off it is an agony.

Friday 2ⁿᵈ February

Went to Saslova with Turner to take food to the Serb who is guarding hospital baggage till the line is clear for traffic. We both put on all the clothes we could carry, but it was no good against the cold, we froze. Since the arrival of the last train, nothing has been able to get through the snow. We got back rather before we meant to, so sauntered through the Thieves' Market. Nothing of interest was to be

---

[1] ie 'The Firm', Brikbeck, Turner and Edwards.

[2] Short for Studebaker

seen on the stalls, but we hung about in the heavy snow where people were selling, and hoped for the priceless treasure that sellers produce from their pocket so often. So far we have had no luck. An orange blouse bought at a second hand clothes stall and a hand carved box, were all we came home with, but quite justified the trip.

Got home just too late to go to the garage.

Thieves' Market

Saturday 3rd February

Colder than ever. Spent the day in bed.

Sunday 4th February

Colder still. 37 degrees frost. Spent a long lazy day under Studdy with Turner. Scratching scratching mud into our eyes, and we warbled our songs, to the accompaniment of our chisels, and to the distraction of the others!

In the evening, wounded were coming in, sledge after sledge, packed in straw. The lying down cases in huge rough box-like sledges. All the time it snowed. They say the fighting has pretty well ceased all along the line owing to the weather. Stores cannot be got up – either food or ammunition.

Mrs Haverfield and Onslow returned from Galatz at 1am. The town is being shelled daily – about four shells dropped into the station and lowest part of it each morning. The English left weeks ago, and most of the inhabitants. The Armoured Car people are there – not doing a lot. The Bulgars have been pushed back a bit, but one wonders why they do not flatten out Galatz.

Tea at Franconi's. The company in despair rather. They want us to sign on a further six months. Teddy and Co are not being invited to. I am – and if I do will be left with just the officers. Mrs Haverfield has to go home to receive 18 drivers. Had a hell of a time in deciding to stick it out.

Monday 5th February

Best news of the stunt. I am to be given a few weeks leave, to go home with the others, and sign on again, to come out with the new draft. Carriage paid both ways. The firm has lost its reason. Leave leave leave, to start anytime.

Tuesday 6th February

The consul rather damped our ardour by forbidding us to go – because of submarines.[1] Feel we can't wait long.

Thursday 8th February

Come to my senses at last, not going on leave – signing on again for another 6 months.

Friday 9th February

Beginning to think I have spent all my life – a very very long one – under Studdy. The chisel has been exchanged for a long lean paintbrush. Grey paint wanders slowly down the handle, and up my sleeve. Some of the complicated corners were worth pocking out, but it's not an enlivening occupation. Crouched round the stove at lunch.

I went to tea with Bell at her Hotel Moscow. The party was Bell, her sister, her nurse, and two men in plain clothes that I supposed to be "consuls". They were firm friends of hers - and that, backed by my sense of humour, was enough to make me invite them to lunch at the garage. It ought to be funny seeing them sharing a box with Marx, and watching her hackles rise at their paltry height and over-done clothes. All the same I feel some agitation at the prospect. Teddy still in bed with flu.[2]

---

[1] In consequence of severence of relations between Germany and the USA on 3 February.

Saturday 10th February

Mrs Haverfield and Onslow left for England in the early morning. Tragedies seem over-common among the S.W.H.[1]

Studdy is very smart. I can't help hoping that when she dies, she'll die on her back, that her lining will show. She won't have long, I fear – her frame is cracked right across. Onslow thinks this happened in a smash at Antwerp, before Studdy retreated her first retreat. Franconi's for Turner and I. We heard some people discussing the end of the war. Everyone says from three to six months, till one has excited oneself into thinking one feels in one's bones some big change coming. We talk of it, always. Everyone does. Meanwhile, in the nearer future, people are betting on the length of the blockade. I am betting on these people being held up three months.

Pain in my head is being very trying.

Turner and I tried for the baths but having picked our way through an immense crowd to the caisse, found we had chosen a 2nd class only day.

Teddy better. It's horrid being ill in a crowd.

The air seems clearer a little from depression by the departures of Mrs Haverfield and Bell.

Orderly duty is wearing me to a thread. One's weeks off pass in a flash and one has hardly realised the blessed relief of having completed one's week before one is told off again.

Today I began again, and set off to get breakfast. Bacon, eggs. Does one ever break an egg without fear of a puncture? I broke my first with great care and deliberation – and felt almost faint when half came away and nothing else happened. You must have yourself been through two retreats and then tried to poach a hard-boiled egg to realize just what a turn it gives. We live well now.

Went to the dentist, with Turner, then to the baths, where they were refusing all but 2nd class bathers. We were turned away dirty and discomfitted – and trudged off to Fanconi's to console ourselves with chocolate and spanking ices.

Sunday 11th February

Washed myself all the morning. It took all that – I hope my hair is at last looking clean again.

---

[2] This paragraph is not in the typescript.

[1] They were to recruit more drivers and talk to the London committee of the S.W.H. about the difficulties between Mrs Haverfield and her drivers

At 2, Miss Harris and D Holman came for Turner and I, and we four and Fitzroy took off in two sledges for Arcadia. It was good going, and lovely when we got there. It does make one long to go with a private horse, at fifteen miles an hour. I felt the whole time that the horses that took us would so far rather not. Nevertheless we went a good rate. Got back to tea with the Harrises. It's such a delightful house to go to. Mrs Harris, French, is charming to all – Mr, an interesting old man of brains, the kind of brains that play bridge and make railways. We stayed on to supper.

With D Holman at Arcadia.

Monday 12ᵗʰ February

Turner and I wandered rather reluctantly to work. The sun was really shining to some purpose and it would have been pleasant to have basked a bit. We dawdled on a wall overlooking the port for a brief half hour. Ice hemmed in the ships and lay as far as the harbour bar.

Why does the sun never shine in the yard of no 10? Gloom meets one and chills one the moment one reaches the arch into the courtyard. Though one does not read it, one <u>feels</u> with force "Abandon hope all ye that enter here" carved over the gate.

Today different from most. It was hardly after 12 before I heard Turner call "Come out" and I found as I crawled out from under the Studdy – the two "consuls" burst upon my vision in all their horror. Clad in immense fur coats, they resembled actors more than anything else. Turner of course having been previously primed and warned played up well. We knocked off at once, and sat round the stove, while the water boiled for lunch. We had a good deal of trouble in smuggling two extra portions of food for them – under the eyes of the evil witch Marx. I had warned her they were coming, but had been frightened out of saying they were coming to lunch! Marx does not make it easy to like her if the chance friends one picks up turn up – as had the consuls. So correct – as I could only suppose, as they were not needing lunch they should have been most welcome.[1] They brought a huge brown paper parcel of food with them – biscuits, sardines, chock and several bottles, port

---

[1] These two sentences interpolated into the typescript.

and champagne! Never before had the garage echoed to the cheerful popping of corks since the S.W. crossed the threshold.

We were pretty conscious of the burning interest of Day and Percy, and what they must be busying their minds with. Just as we were junketing Marx turned up, and my promises to myself were fulfilled.

Marx even refused to notice my friends' worth until I showed her the loot. One tin sardines, three rolls of biscuits, one box of chocks, one tin chocolate and milk. That should brighten our lives for many meals to come.

Don't care _what_ Marx says, they _are_ nice consuls. They were practically shovelled out of the door by Marx, hurling invitations to Turner and I over their shoulders. They are taking a flat, it seems. We shouted delighted acceptances after them, to Marx's horror, as she indignantly protested she would have to refuse. Certainly she must do her own dirty work, if the S.W.H. are such infernal snobs.

Tuesday 13th February

Turner and I went down to the Port to repack, sort and tabulate the tents of the unit. It was a terrific job, and bitterly cold. We worked in greatcoats and gloves.

Hones, the Berrys' orderly, helped us and six Serbs did the hauling and packing. We got along well, but it's the kind of job I loathe. Hones gave us a good lunch in his cupboard, and delicious cigs. Will we ever settle down quietly and naturally to being front door people again? As chauffeurs we _are_ chauffeurs, and our lot falls with them, and that class. It's all an immensely interesting question, and where one does really belong. Either – nowhere – or everywhere –

The port was partly frozen only. I photographed brazenly and was as I thought en train de being arrested by a ferocious-looking officer when a Berry ambulances whisked us off home.

Tea at Franconi's with Turner. The cakes get smaller and smaller.

Wednesday 14th February

Down to the port again. A luggage sledge was going down with stores so Turner and I went as passengers. The man allowed me to drive his two very scraggy nags, and I made an alarming attempt which failed and nearly landed us on the pavement. Frost again after the thaw has reduced the roads to absolutely sheet ice. It was a miracle to me that our horses could keep on their feet at all. The whole long sledge with fixed pole would slide out at an angle, away from one horse, and cutting under the legs of the other. Horses were down at several corners. It is particularly painful to see their efforts to get up again on the ice.

The port was more closed in than ever. Our job was to paint number of tent and contents of bag on each. With lots of white paint to splash about we were thoroughly happy till we knocked off for lunch. The sun was shining so we took it out and explored – we prowled along inside the sea wall till we found a break and found - on the other side – a peaceful little sandy beach. It was a great surprise for on the other side are all railway lines, wharves and a pack of boats in the harbour. Here along the sand gulls walked and sunned themselves at leisure. A little flock of duck were riding on the top of the waves too.

Turner and I crawled along the broken boulders of the old wall, as far as we dared. It was extremely slippery, but we crept on till we reached the Teddy Bear Cave, which we discovered the other day. They tell great tales of happenings four years ago. The ladies of Odessa could never venture out alone, for fear of being kidnapped by brigands who carried them off to these caves, and held them there till generous merchants came to their aid and bartered silk and other treasures for them.[1]

Shooting scandal in Franconi's.

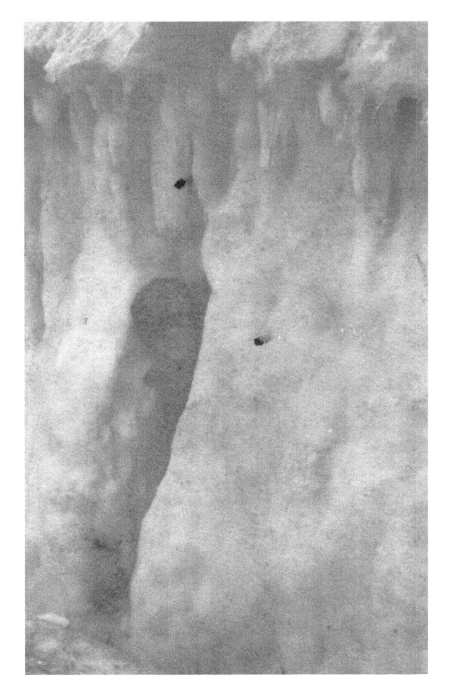

The Teddy
Bear Cave.

---

[1] These two sentences are interpolated into the typescript.

Thursday 15th February

Worked hard at the garage and enjoyed myself jointly putting up the back axle with Percy. We raced over each bolt and I won, most times. Turner and I to tea at Franconi's after. We go now from force of habit, not any longer because it amuses us. I met Fitzroy at the dentist afterwards and we both went through untold horror.

The Baby Burford at 10, Sofiaskian.

Friday 16th February

Garage, alone. Too cold and miserable to work, so huddled over the stove till time for my dentist again. He is a very interesting person – looks like a priest, in a long white overall to his feet. He talked of many things and among others of interest, the end of the war. When I asked his reasons for his optimistic prophecies he merely said, "My child, in Russia just now are many things of which one does not speak – and in that he told me what he meant. The word that no one breathes above a whisper.

Saturday 17th February

We are all standing on our heads again, not knowing whether or not to go or stay.

Last night Teddy and Turner went with Tchaikoff on the bust. Marx let them go to a cinema, but they went on to dinner and a concert at an "Officers' Club". They came in at 20 to 12. Marx was at the opera so nothing happened till next day. There was of course an all round strafe. I told Marx it was entirely her own fault for being so silly as to let them go. Anyone could have told her that those two with or without Tchaikoff would do something idiotically unbefitting a Scottish Woman.

As always occurs in units such as ours, their attitude has been the cause of many and stringent new rules, and I expect Tchaikoff will go the way of my consuls. What a life –

Hedges turned up from Reni, for home – the last of the Buffs, bar the evil witch of Marx. I must go too. It's best, only very very hard to make up my mind. Anyway I must and <u>will</u> come out – again – if possible.

Sunday 18th February.

Busy.

Monday 19th February

Put in a plea at the consulate for passes, and been sent home to give written reasons for returning. The real one being a wish to see the old man. They were all triumphs but mine I think took the prize. It was awfully hard to think of any reason that could not be used to prevent me rejoining, and thus ending my career for ever as a Scottish Woman. Ill health and so on were barred, so I merely said I wished to go as I wasn't wanted for the next two months at least. Marx certified to the truth of the statement and we waited breathlessly till Walker returned to say they were considered fairly respectable.

Wednesday 21st February

Cold and tired.

Thursday 22nd February

Still waiting for news.

Tchaikoff haunts us. His post of "administrator" to the Greek shower does not provide him with enough work. A nervous breakdown necessitated his getting some such appointment. The illness has left him energetic and irritable. He has plunged into a frantic admiration for Walker with all the energy of a two year old. The firm derive endless satisfaction there from.[1] Her illness has reduced him to frenzy. Today he turned out of his room for her. During meals – at all times in season and out - he comes trotting in and out to talk to us. It has become a habit to come while we have supper and sit and talk till we all dribble off to bed. Usually some little treasure wrapped up in paper is brought – an old coin – a Roman remain – a bit of shrapnel from his boot – and so on. He is of course really kind and interesting. Sometimes the Co. can induce him to rake up stories from his past – his seven duels kept us going for some time, though the stories we felt would have pleased us most were 'des secrets'.

Marx took out the touring car and hung herself up somewhere – and was towed in by Ilneachenko, a good friend on the last retreat. Marx brought him to have tea, and he and I arranged to exchange lessons – Russian and English. He came back after supper, and was terribly earnest over his English. I can only hope the reason he learnt so much more than I did was that I teach better than he does - he talked very bad German, and no French, and was full of talk of Russia. Many things I heard of the Russian army that one has heard before, but surprise one by the telling each time. His own adventures were exciting too. He was cut off at the Tulcea-Isaccea road the day after we got through, and after three days in a Turkish camp he and his sergeant escaped – one night when his guards were drunk. Their battery he got through somehow before the bridge was bombed and went back with a lorry for some reason – and so it was he was caught. For his performance there he has got the highest decoration given. This last I heard from L.S. He left at 10.

Friday 23rd February

Garage colder than ever – obviously too cold for work there.

Saturday 24th February

Sun but minus 35 degrees. Turner and I went to our garage but it made us feel sick. Day, Turner and I sat round the stove and he told us some of his best stories, illustrating his own low cunning in deaing with swindling landladies and bankrupt customers. He is satisfactorily true to type.

---

[1] These four senences are interpolated in the typescript.

Returned to find a note and a letter, one to say we have got passes for England, the other to say the old man is dead – a grim joke on the part of Providence.

Sunday 25th February

Pottered. Dr Klegg came to tea. Marx gave an opera party for the last bust. She took two boxes. The party were two Englishmen, Mr Jerome, Illneachenko, Robin, Dr Klegg, Teddy Bear & Co[1], and Marx. It was fearfully funny. Illneachenko came at 6 for his lesson, and we struggled on till supper, when happily Mr Jerome arrived and of course spoke Russian – we have no common language. Tchaikoff strolled in and complicated matters further. We found Illneachenko's lorry outside and he drove us all to the opera in it. The opera *Cherivibski* was really a delightful fairytale, full of witches, devils and such like. The appearance and disappearance of the devil thrilled us far more than the music. Someone even flew out of the chimney in a temper and put the moon in his pocket. To boil down the whole plot, it was the story of a peasant in love with a girl who refused to marry him unless he would give her the shoes the emperess wore. He had complicated matters previously by incurring the ill will of the devil, by drawing an uncomplimentary picture of him on the church door. With the help of the devil, who he outwitted and defeated, he went off in search of the shoes and returned triumphant – only to be told she did not care a rap for the shoes, but wanted him only. Rather a frost for the young man after his dangerous ride on the back of the devil to fetch them for her. The peasants' costumes were lovely.

I was pushed off with Illneachenko to see what I could do for the Firm in the way of souveneering. I failed signally and rejoined the others, Teddy and Co and Dr Klugg, to report on my failure. He was a good deal horrified and whipped off two of his a.c. badges for T and I at once.

I got dreadfully tired of Illneachenko and longed to be with the others.

We all clambered into the lorry when the show ended, and Illneachenko buzzed us off to "Little Fountain" and back. He drove beautifully, and very very fast over a hideous road. We all rattled about inside like peas in a drum and ended up here at 12.20. They all came in for coffee, and the evening's amusement nearly ended in a duel. Mr Jerome however saved the situation and removed Illneachenko, vowing vengeance on Tchaikoff and his servants, who, he said, had insulted him and us.

---

[1] That is, Birkbeck, Edwards and Turner.

Monday 26th February

No work – no more here ever again. Pottered about with a funny detached feeling of having nothing special to do. After being in the grip of the S.W.H. for six months it felt odd indeed. Bought a lovely enamel match box. Had tea at Franconi's. Pretty full. Dr Klugg and co. there. We sat near a big smart Cossack who turned out to be drunk – kind waiter shifted us before the row began.

We were all marshalled at the consulate, those who were for home - Brown, Bowerman, Hedges and the Firm - and all were asked what we were going to do when we got home – and having been already primed, we said with one voice, "War work." The chorus made even Mr Bagge laugh.

Tuesday 27th February

Another thaw. We went to Sofiaskian 10 for the last time and spent an hour with Day round the stove. It gave me the creeps rather, saying goodbye to all the poor plucky little ambulances. It may be au revoir but one never knows.

We went on to say goodbye to Mr and Mrs Sadnikoff. They are a nice pair.

Lunched with the Bagges and spent the day pottering and packing.

Thursday 1st March

Spent the day doing things for the last time. Tea at Franci's. We stayed late and on returning home found Messrs Jerome, Klugg and Illneachenko here, to say goodbye – the latter laden with badges. He says he is also going to Petrograd. We begged the others to come too. Hated saying goodbye to them all. People all count so on a stunt like this.

11. Petrograd: 2nd – 18th March.

11. Petrograd: 2nd – 18th March.

Friday 2nd March

Turner, Teddy, Hedges, Walker, Brown, Bowerman and myself left for England. Tchaikoff and four of his menials came with us to the station. We all went down in the Selden – one of the wretched soldiers carrying an enormous flower garden, Tchaikoff's last gift to Walker. Several of the sisters came to see us off. Tchaikoff delighted the Firm by making a spectacle of himself on the platform. One of the Berrys' sisters came too, and shared a cabin with the Firm. Old, but not at all bad. Mile after mile of flat open counrty till it grew dark. After supper we sang and that brought four R. officers hurrying to the door. We had not much use for them, but it took us two hours to show it. One sang duets with Hedges with great effect.

At night when the moon rose we were passing through forest again. The moonlight shadow cave of the fir trees in the snow, is as near fairyland as one gets nowadays I think.

Saturday 3rd March

Woke late. The night had been very hot and a good wash in icy water was most refreshing. We had tea for breakfast and ate nothing till lunchtime. From 2 till 6 we stopped at _____ Ice in huge blocks was being shipped off. It was a lovely greenish colour. Another sing song after supper.

Sunday 4th March

At Shlobin when we woke – and there we stayed till 4. 20. Went out and walked up and down for an hour or two, never knowing when the train would leave. It was bitterly cold, though the sun was brilliant. The snow underfoot was solid crust ice. Many troops were on the move, as usual in fearfully crowded trains.

Monday 5th March

Another sunny day. The train really hurried along at last. In the afternoon we passed many little villages that reminded us very much of Norway. It snowed again. At 4 we arrived at Petrograd where we were met by a Red Cross man. While we were waiting I had a long talk twith two of our fellow travellers – one a French woman, the other a Romanian. Somewhat to my surprise the former took a very bitter point of view of the part England had played in the war. She said that the war would only end when we were ready, and that we would not be ready till Germany was smashed – but added that if we wished it we could smash her tomorrow. Her argument was that we had all the wealth of the world, and wealth is might. The other was hot in defence of my country and told her what we had done. I asked her what other country could have made an army such as ours in two years. The Romanian said our soldiers were fighting men and sportsmen, and that we should win. Being a Romanian of course he had to add that. He said we three were an illustration of the sporting instinct of our country.

Six sledges conveyed us and our luggage to an hotel – Teddy and I, rather thrilled, bringing up the rear. The Hotel Select turned out to be far more pleasing than we had expected. We three were delighted with the room we shared. A sitting room – with our bedroom paraphenalia in a little curtained-off alcove. Dined sumptuously, had baths and went to bed – thoroughly content with the world.

Tuesday 6th March

Petrograd indeed. The firm breakfasted on its own, and then set out in a snowstorm to explore the great city. Really one never gets used to sledges being taken seriously. Always at the back of my mind I expect someone to say there isn't enough snow really – and I see the donkey harnessed to the tea-tray – but to see people like one's Father skidding about in them is still a little odd. We saw a funeral and a fire engine on runners, the latter drawn by four beautiful blacks. All along the Nevsky Prospect we trudged, gasping at the length and breadth of the street.

At tea we met Moir, Grant, Alice and Reaney who had been hung up seven weeks, but leave for England tomorrow. They had all been shoved into nursing homes or charity institutions – and we consider ourselves most lucky in our quarters. We heard of most of the others en route for home, scattered over the country between here and Bergen – winter sporting – and putting up at the best hotels - at the expense of S.W.H. Paid two calls of promise and tramped home quite tired to our hotel. The peace of our sitting room cannot be described.

Aroused at 12.15 for a telephone call. Teddy answered it. _____,[1] Armoured Cars – has sent an invitation to lunch with him tomorrow.

The firm speculated on what the morrow might bring forth, and on other matters, till 3 am.

Wednesday 7th March

Breakfast at 10, and then we leisurely dressed and drove off to the Astoria. Here our host burst upon us as rather a shock. While he was cichassing, we sat in the lounge and watched with huge amusement the passing show. The gayest sparks of officers strolled up and down under the palms – Russian, Italian, Belgian, Romanian, French – all in their faultless uniforms and boots suggesting rather comic opera, than war. We lunched a little party of four, and it turned out rather a surprise. No doubt we burst upon our host as even a greater shock in our short khaki frocks – when he was no doubt expecting pearl necklaces and silk stockings. However he bore up well and the conversation ran in interesting if rather dangerous channels.

After lunch he and a friend took us to see after a job they had on hand, and then dropped us here – at 6. The firm were very satisfied and hope for more. Bitterly cold.

Murphy came to dinner at her own invitation – but we were not having any.

Thursday 8th March[2]

Spent idle morning. After lunch we went to the Russian peasant shops. Turner left us to scrape up some old relations. Teddy and I lost our heads badly amongst the birds in both shops. They are the quaintest little things imaginable, carved quite roughly in wood, more or less on kingfisher lines, and painted fierce reds and blue and green, splashed with gold. I also bought a jolly jug. Coming home the lid unfortunately got knocked off, and broken. We got into a crowd – bread riots we were later told – and got pushed through shop window – in the rush of the crowd, to avoid the charge of cossacks.

---

[1] The name is very blackly crossed out.

[2] International Women's Day – the unofficial strike by women textile factory workers spread to Putilov arms works and other industries, and ended by involving 90,000 workers – the start of the Russian Revolution. The final sentence of this paragraph is added to the typescript.

224

Friday 9th March

All went to the Red Cross commissioner for our passports. He held out hopes of getting us off to Christiana soon, but not to England. Coming home heard a new tune – and saw some magnificent Cossacks – and made a new friend – Hazelwoods – English in hotel - – one does "abroad". Stayed in after lunch.

Saturday 10th March

Teddy has too bad a cold to go out, so Turner and I went with our friends as arranged yesterday. Snowing again. We drove off first to the Cathedral, a wonderful compact kind of church of precious pillars, malachite and lapis lazuli. The icons were studded with jewels. The doors of moulten bronze. Altogether such a Church as would impress the Russian mind with the importance and splendour of their gods. Next we drove to the Church of the Resurrection – the church we had called the lollypop church, because of its many domes, striped pink, green, blue. Inside the promise was more than fulfilled – walls and roof were one mass of mosaic. It made me a little giddy. Under a canopy supported by jasper pillars one saw the spot on the road on which the Emperor Alexander II had been murdered. Whether the church was built as a thank-offering for his death or his life we did not arrive at.

Lunch next – at the Café de Paris – and a very good lunch too. We sat opposite a glass, and I smiled at the reflection of our party: Turner, Messrs Bennett, Blake and myself. The museum of Alexander – a collection of Russian art – two modern paintings by Borisov I loved. The rest were wasted on me completely. A circulatory route brought us home at 3.

All 3 dined with Edward Jacquier – 7.30. He was alone in his little flat, and it was all very comfortable and peaceful. Everything – his pipe – his fire – and his armchair – all all reminded me of lots of things that used to happen and made me wish never to see England again, more fervently than usual. He told us many amusing stories and was altogether a very entertaining and amusing young man, especially when he talked of his own particular job – money. Absolutely all lack of proportion has gone for the time being. The telephone rang twice during dinner, giving warnings of his coming death –warnings he laughed off. [1]

We drove off home at 10 through almost empty streets, long white streets, the lamps in straight lines, in perspective on and on to a vanishing point. The sledge glided along silently till the hollow wooden echo told us we were crossing a bridge. The whole city seems to be cut up by canals, frozen now, with poor dead looking barges in the grip of the ice.

Sunday 11th March

Turner and I went out after lunch to see what was happening and found immense crowds, surging up and down the Nevsky.[2] A general strike is on – opposite the Nicolai Station the police were loosing off into the crowd with a machine gun. Bands of Cossacks rode up and down, pretending to do the same, but charged along, firing into the air. People got hit. Someone inside a house opened fire at the crowd who hurried into areas and courtyards. At one point the crowd were pressing towards the Nevsky and Turner and I got onto a goods sledge to see what would happen just as someone was shot, and we found ourselves alone in possession of the Ligovskaya! There were campfires in the Nevsky and army posts. After that we decided the Select might be the best place after all. Messrs Blake and Bennett[3] joined us after dinner and we did gymnastic feats.

Monday 12th March

All shops shut. All day we prowled about. We have just realised the importance of things, viz, neither bread riots or anti-war motive are putting through the rebellion – and such it is all right. Today the soldiers have gone over entirely to the revolutionaries, and are only seen scattered through the crowd. All officers have had their swords taken from them, and soldiers and civilians alike are armed with rifles, revolvers or daggers. Any droshkies still about are being held up, the passengers turned out, and the driver sent home. All cars are comandeered by the revolutionists who crowd aboard them. All wear red favours, and all appear to be in the hands of the people. During the day there was much shooting. Blake took the firm out after dinner, but we had not got far before we were in the thick of a fight. Two army lorries full of soldiers and armed civilians were fired upon, from a house held by the police in the Ligovskaya. The lorries replied with volley after volley and

---

[1] The second half of this sentence is added to the typescript.

[2] The army was called in to control the crowds; many regiments mutinied. They turned against the police, who were firing machine-guns concealed on rooftops. The Tzar dissolved the Duma, but its members refused to leave the building, and waited in an adjoining room to take control.

[3] Naval engineers hurrying home from their assignment in China. Leonard J Blake was to marry Turner.

a fierce fight raged for some time. We meanwhile had all fled like most of the crowd into a courtyard opposite, where we got an excellent view in comparative safety. On the stroke of midnight cars and lorries scattered copies of the manifest of the new liberal government, to the crowd. It was met with cheer after cheer. Some kind of mass meeting was taking place in the square.

We returned at 2am. The hall was still full of anxious people, wandering about consulting in the dark. One told us that Milyukov was at the head of the liberals. The cry of the crowd was down with the German woman. Returned to our room for tea – saying as usual what wonderful people the Russians are. Fairly quiet night.

Tuesday 13th March

Congratulating the Russians on having got through their troubles very quietly, and ourselves on having kept our whole skins – when a great deal of noise outside our hotel and an absolute fusillade at the corner made us wonder what was coming next. We leapt up and dressed in record time. Then the revolutionaries poured into the hotel. Every room was searched. Some one had fired from one of the windows – and they meant business. Such a mob as poured into our room – soldiers, factory hands, old men and young – all carrying firearms or knives. We cordially welcomed our visitors (never annoy a man with a gun) – and gave them cigarettes. After a rapid glance round the room, they saluted, and clattered off. One of the party was wearing an officer's belt and sword, and got rather entangled with the straps. We fixed him up properly, and were rewarded with the ribbon off his sword. The servants all cleared off, and no food was to be had. "Daddy and Blakie" saved the lives of the firm by getting several yards of sausages and some brown beans. They lunched with us, we contributed soup to the repast. Several times the room was searched by similar parties. It was not till the evening when a second shot was fired from the hotel, that the police officer was discovered on the 3rd floor. He shot himself.

Spent a good deal of time in the hall. Many people left the hotel, thinking it a particularly unhealthy spot. Manyy Russians remained, and hated it. They huddled together in frightened groups and made each other miserable by repeating rumours. The favourite was that the hotel would be blown up in the night.

The Revolutionaries took over the top floor and sentires were placed on each landing. Rather dangerous people. One let off his rifle by mistake outside our door, in the afternoon, and another upstairs during the night. When we were washing up the tea things some of the waiters came back – one wearing a sword – No work done by the servants, so the firm set to at once on a cleaning stunt, and did the rooms of some old ladies. At night a new crowd came in – Revolutionary leaders we think. We now fly a red flag from the hotel door. Sat late in the hall without lights. One's loath to go to bed these days. Fairly persistent shooting all night.

Wednesday 14th March

A fairly quiet night. Woke as usual to hear the occasional pop of a rifle, but everything is quieter. Lorries and cars still tour the city, bristling with armed men – many carrying a machine gun. As many as there is room for crowd into the cars – usually two soldiers lie along the wings, ready to pot at anything or anyone at a moment's notice.

A proclamation of the new government ordered everyone back to work in twenty-four hours. Temporary police are appointed – civilians wearing white brassards[1] with T.I. on them. One or two shops re-opened, and everywhere one sees signs of excellent organisation. The firm street-gazed with Blake. Rumours of course abound. All along the Nevsky are bullet holes and a bomb hole too. We went to see how the Astoria had fared as Military H.Q.. All the ground floor windows are smashed - the curtains, torn and draggled, trail in the snow outside. By the door was a huge heap of wine bottles – we heard there was not a bottle drunk - and the remains of a bonfire of papers. It is now the headquarters of the sailors. Peeping through the windows – barricaded by chairs and tables – it was too odd to see civilian soldiers on guard in the hall among the palm trees where so much gayer uniforms had strolled, last time we were here.

While we were there we heard a strafe in the Nevsky, and by the time we got back there, there was no crowd, just the remains of some unfortunate splashed against the wall. It does not do to lose sight of the force behind it all these days.

No restaurants open in the ordinary way. The Café d'Europe was giving out food and tea to soldiers. We, by virtue of our brassards, were served with tea, for which no money was accepted. It was interesting to see soldiers and officers sitting together at the same table.

After dinner we went out and watched a large fire outside one of the police stations, on which documents were being burnt. An odd sight in the moonlight.

On returning we were hailed with much enthusiasm – and learnt that England and France have wired to say they were in accord with the new government (as English we are hugely popular). Who could fail to be in accord with a government that stands for Freedom of Speech, Freedom of Religion, Liberty of Conscience, Universal Suffrage, and the Responsibility of Ministers? Rumours abound – the abdication of the Tzar is rumoured.

Thursday 15th March

---

[1] Armbands. They themselves were wearing their S.W.H. uniforms and armbands.

Things really quiet today. All have returned to work. Watched a rather thrilling march past of soldiers – their officers again at their head – mostly wearing, like their men, the red flag. How the crowd cheered. Later after tea we saw two lorries of English blue jackets. They were stopped near us and we had a talk to them. The crowd were very enthusiastic and cheered them supposing they had come to help the revolution. We had a little of the reflected glory and got cheered ourselves.

The republic is now officially declared. The Tzar has abdicated.[1] What a country. Tzar's insignia and paintings removed, by Milyukov and Co, in Petrograd.

The latest casulty list does not exceed six thousand – and in three days all appears as usual under the new and excellent regime.

Friday 16th March

Today is devoted to removing all signs of the late monarchy. All signs over shops etc with the Royal Arms are taken down or draped with red. We all went out – Daddy fell to my lot, and I had a tough time of it. We tramped for miles and had a soul-searching conversation on the Empire. Interesting, but I'd rather not. Danced after dinner as usual – the firm does now, it's the latest craze.

This piece of lace is pinned into the diary at this point – a souvenir of the Astoria, perhaps?

Saturday 17th March

Had a board meeting to decide whether Blake shall be admitted into the firm. He was ... and solemnly presented with a skull ring, the insignia of the firm.

Danced again. We three were quietly dancing when a crowd of Russians and Roumanians poured in, we thought for a political meeting and were clearing out, when they barred the way, saying they had come to dance with us. Rather hot stuff, one quite quite mad.

---

[1] In in favour of his brother Michael, who placed power in the hands of the people.

Sunday 18th March

In bed all day – cough. Blakie and Co came round and we all chatted all the afternoon. Got up after dinner and danced. Same crowd – they rather bored us – at least failed to amuse or interest.

Perhaps the part that sits up and takes notice is dead.

Nous verrons.

12: The journey home: from 24th March

12: The journey home: from 24th March

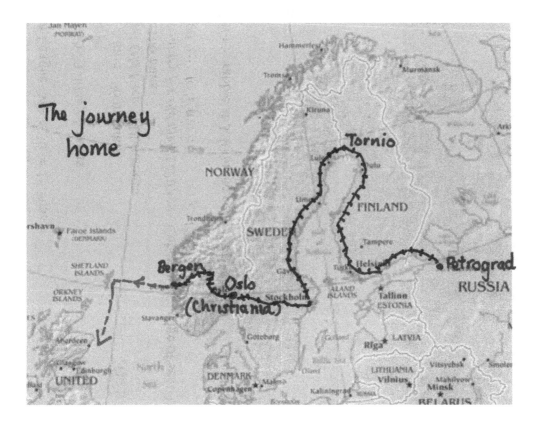

The dated entries end there. There are also four pages of political notes on thin Hotel Select paper: the text of the Tzar's abdication speech, a revolutionary leader's speech, and jottings of what is happening day by day. Perhaps Birkbeck felt it was too dangerous to put in her diary.

We know part of the end of the story, how the party got home, only from Bowerman's diaries. Bowerman dined with Miss Henderson on Thursday 22nd March, at a new restaurant in Petrograd, and Birkbeck and Edwards were also there (was Turner away cementing her friendship with Blake?). On 24th March, Bowerman, Brown, Hedges, Walker and the Firm left Petrograd by train, at 7.40 am, and arrived at Tornio on the Finnish / Swedish frontier, at 12 noon on the 25th, then drove in a sleigh over the river. The big luggage had not yet arrived, and the Firm stayed the night in Tornio to wait for it, while Bowerman's party went on to Christiania (Oslo). 'Birkbeck and Co' arrived there in the evening of 28th March, and met up with the others just in time for Bowerman's party to take the luggage on board their morning train for Bergen. The wording suggests that the Firm remained in Christiania. If there was winter sporting going on, we can be sure they would have joined in. However perhaps homesickness drove them on to do as the earlier parties did: a boat from Bergen, a halt perhaps in Lerwick, but no permission to go ashore, and a landing at last in Aberdeen, Edinburgh or Newcastle. Birkbeck might just have made it in time for her sister Judith's wedding, on the 17th April 1917; it would be some weeks more before she heard of the death of her brother Gervase, in a prisoner of war camp in Gaza, Palestine, on 20th April 1917.

Meanwhile, Marx had written a letter to the London Committee of the S.W.H. in which she said that the driving conditions in Romania were too difficult for women, and so, when Birkbeck tried to sign on once more, permission was refused. Hedges, however, returned as a "laundry Supervisor". Dr Inglis was furious, and threatened to withdraw the whole enterprise if it was not fully staffed by women; the London Committee re-thought, but by that time Birkbeck was driving in France.

On 20th March 1917, the members of the Unit were formally presented with the Serbian St George medal, 4th class, for Bravery under fire. They were particularly pleased that the medals were the same as those given to male soldiers. The medals were silver, with the Tzar on one side, and "For Valour" on the other. One diarist remarked that they had to be worn 'inside-out'; if not, the wounded soldiers would gently turn them, to hide the Tzar's head.

Some of the Unit, Birkbeck among them, were also presented with the medal of St Stanislaus, for a act of particular bravery – in Birkbeck's case, the incident where she changed her tyre during the aeroplane bombardment of Medgidia.

The Unit remained in Russia until November, leaving only when Dr Inglis had ensured the safety of the remaining Serbian soldiers. Under pressure from her, the War Office at last recalled the Serbian Divisions, meaning to send them to Salonica. By this time Dr Inglis was very ill with stomach cancer, and she died on 26th November, the day after their arrival in Newcastle. She was the first woman to be presented with the Order of the White Eagle with Swords, Serbia's highest honour.

Marsali Taylor 2011:

Why did she stop writing? There's a good third of the book left, and she'd kept a diary ever since she was a girl. Was it the piles of burning papers outside the police stations? She could have been afraid her notebooks would have been seized as political papers, or even, given her writing, the ciphers of a spy. She was uncharacteristically quiet about their arrest on 11th March; perhaps being on the 'wrong' side, even for a short time, shook her, and gave her the sense of what was coming, when Russian public opinion was to turn against the Scottish women for their habits of walking out among the trenches and riding through the countryside, and several Unit members were in real danger of being shot.

Perhaps, more simply, she felt that the adventure was over. She was only 26; she'd lived through excitement, hardship, illness, danger and being set aside for a male mechanic, and now, on the way home to all that was familiar, a revolution. Perhaps she'd just had enough.

Douglas Gordon Baxter, 1991:

The last entry ends: Mais nous verrons.

Aunt Ysabel did wait and saw within weeks that her help was needed in France, Enlisting with FANY[1], she took herself to the battlefields there, doing once more what she did best, driving back and forward to the front bringing out wounded.

When the war ended she had now added to the Serbian medals of St Stanislaus and St George. The citation records her service "as an ambulance driver with the Allied armies during more than two years in Russia, Romania, and then in France, showing courage and coolness during operations around Château Thierry, Noyon and then Verdun, where she had particularly distinguished herself on 23 and 24 October 1918 in continuing to transport wounded under violent bombardment." for which she was awarded the Croix de Guerre with Bronze Star.

Later it was said of her that "there cannot be many women who won the Croix de Guerre with Bronze Star in the first World War" and that "she was a formidable sight at British Legion parades with her two rows of medals."

After the Great War she lived alone in a cottage in the middle of a wood near Raynham, Norfolk, to recover one feels from all that had been seen and done. This nature therapy, if such it was, continued until her iron will and robust constitution had sufficiently healed the scars of war, and the events of the past had sufficiently healed to allow her inherent disposition to believe again that life is for living, and that one must extract from life all that life can afford. This proved stronger in the end than times past, and it sent her out to Tangier, to marriage at Khartoum, and a new life with her District Commissioner husband at Talodi in south central Sudan.

---

[1] First Aid Nursing Yeomanry

Hard on her arrival, as if not wishing to disappoint her thirst for military adventures, and to keep her hand in, as it were, the 10th Sudanese batallion stationed there mutinied after the assassination of the Governor General of the Sudan, broke into the ammunition store, looted it, and for some days bullets whizzed and richochetted around her head, but just when things were beginning to look really interesting, as dawn broke some days later, the cavalry, or anyway, rescuers, arrived over the horizon in true Beau Geste / Gaumont British style to put an end to what for some was bloody insurrection, WAR, but for Aunt Ysabel it amounted to no more than a sudden slight turbulence of the atmosphere, a little touch of déjà vu, as they say.

After some years they moved to Lalyo in the extreme south of the Sudan, a little more than four degrees north of the equator, in hill country. But the Gods which had looked after her in time of war, which she hated, were perversely unable to extend their cover to a time of peace, which she loved, and with Byzantine cunning decreed that she would have to go, as the antidote to blackwater fever was unknown even to them. Or so they said, whereas to restore the usual cover to her while she saved Londoners was comparatively easy, and would soon be needed.

It was a wrench. She made it clear she would never have left, save for her life, and those of others, but went reluctantly, a decision always bitterly regretted. Careless of her health to a degree almost suicidal, the implications of living in the Sudan and 'having to take care' where adventuring, expeditions and endless safaris were the breath of life, was an insupportable interference, and not the stuff of which successful expeditions were made at all.

The nostalgia she always felt for the Sudan made it clear that she never would have left otherwise, for she loved the country, the native people, the landscape, the diversity of the wildlife, the climate in the hills above 1500 feet, and the life she lived there.

She lived for a few years in Kent until, in 1940, 'she ran to London', she said, when she heard 'that others were running away from London', to join the Mechanised Transport Corps as an ambulance driver to take up once more the rescue from this new front, at home, of the dead and dying from the smoking rubble of their houses as the bombs pounded the city night after night, and flaming buildings crashed to the ground around her during the London Blitz. This too she did with that 'courage and coolness' which had so distinguished her earlier, and was rewarded with similar recognition by her country.

She continued by working for the YWCA in Belgium and Germany with the British Women's Services there, before becoming a civilian again in 1946, able to take up those things for herself that had been so long ago laid aside, but never abandoned even in the direst moments as can be seen in sketches from the Russian front as bombs burst around her. Painting, sketching, and the study of nature in all its forms, particularly fungi superbly illustrated in great detail and about which she became an acknowledged expert.

The call of Caolas Mor all this time had proved irresistable and it was to there she went increasingly. When her husband died suddenly she moved after his death from London to a double garden flat at Douglas Crescent, Edinburgh, where the worst of the winter months were spent, but for most of the year her true, her spiritual, home was Caolas Mor, as it always had been.

Marsali Taylor, 2011:

Dad sees her differently from the way I do. Coolness, courage, determination; yes, she had all those, but reading the diaries, looking at the photos, I see the bunch of laughing girls who washed their hair in buckets on a barge, flirted with officers and, when the time came, drove doggedly through mud and over stones, gritting their teeth against the screams of the wounded until their task was accomplished.

I would like to think I could have been there with them, if my time had come then.

Aunt Ysabel is a part of our lives still. After her death, when I was a teenager, we bought the house in Douglas Crescent from her son Neil. He left the diaries with Dad so her story would be written, and left, too, almost all of the items in the house. Her Russian icon of St Nicholas, bought perhaps by Turner or Teddy as a Christmas present for her in that Odessa market, hangs in my sister's house near Brora; the kingfisher box from Petrograd sits on the top of Mum's china cabinet. On the Centenary Women's March in Edinburgh 2009, I wore her Red Cross Transport badge.

Here's how the diaries end:

This is a tale of damsels Three
Turner, Edwards and Birkbeck we
Birkbeck is Bruin, named before
She came to this land of snow
Where bears are many, & Birkbecks few
(Such are not found in any Zoo.)
Edwards is Teddie, what else could she be?
And Turner completes the Company
Of Teddie, Bear and Co!

We have wandered round in Russia,
Down into Roumania too —
Had adventures big & little
And misfortunes not a few.
(Other folk will tell you so.)
But we rise above disaster
Jehu-like we drive the faster
Teddie, Bear and Co!

When we worked in far Dobrudja
bringing Fords up at the front
Life was rather hectic sometimes
Wasn't quite a "cushy" stunt
(When the work was ended, Oh!)
English Russians, all have scanned us
Was there one who could withstand us
Teddie, Bear, & Co?

Arm in arm we stormed Odessa
"Jove to think" the folks at Faucs.
Made glad eyes at all & sundry
Mowed them down like British "tanks"
(Just a hint to let you know)
All the Russkys have adored us
Serbs & Cossacks — all applaud us
Teddie Bear, and Co!

Now we're stuck in Petrogradsky
(All things Russian end like that)
We have stopped the old aspersions
Cast upon the English "Miss"
Sometimes folks have called her slow!
All this nonsense has been altered
Never once the "firm" has faltered.
Teddie, Bear, and Co!

Soon we'll cross the sea to England
Say goodbye to all things flighty.
We'll shed a silent tear
When we see the coast of "Blighty".
But my friends, I'd have you know
We shall never be downhearted
For the "firm" can NOT be parted
Teddie, Bear and Co!

———————— " ————————

N.M.

Petrograd 19/3/17.

1

_____ and

the War Horse

said

"Ha -

-Ha!"

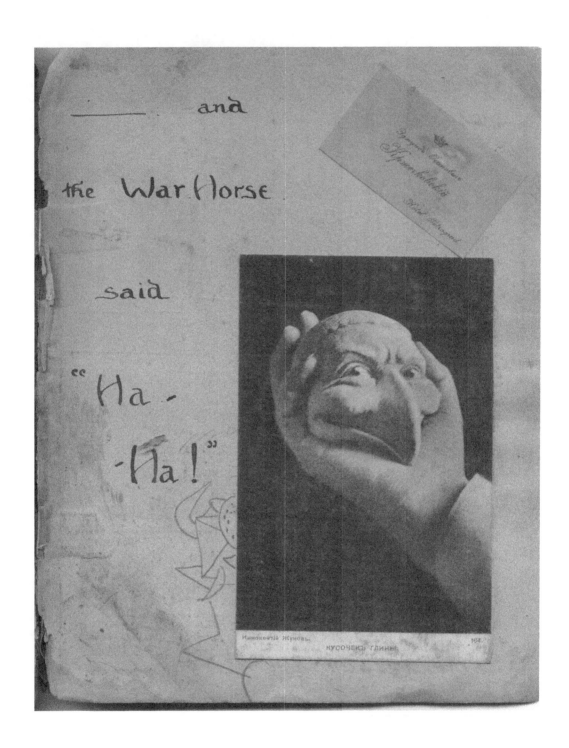

I didn't know Aunt Ysabel's story when she was alive to ask; but what could that child have asked? How could Birkbeck have fitted that heroic enterprise into a child's understanding? Instead, she taught me what she'd learnt about endurance: 'Go on till you can't do any more, and then do another hundred bucketfuls.'